THE CARIBBEAN

THE CARIBBEAN

CULTURE OF RESISTANCE,
SPIRIT OF HOPE

Edited by Oscar L. Bolioli

Friendship Press · **New York**

Editorial Offices:
475 Riverside Drive, New York, NY 10115

Distribution Offices:
P.O. Box 37844, Cincinnati, OH 45222-0844

Manufactured in the United States of America

Library of Congress Cataloging-in-Publication Data

The Caribbean : culture of resistance, spirit of hope / edited by
Oscar Bolioli
    p. cm.
    Includes bibliographical references.
    ISBN 0-377-00254-2
    1. Caribbean Area—Social conditions. 2. Church and social
problems—Caribbean Area. I. Bolioli, Oscar.
HN193.5.C37   1993
261.8'09729—dc20   92-43635
                                    CIP

Contents

UNITED STATES

GULF OF MEXICO

THE BAHAMAS

TURKS AND CAICOS

CUBA

MEXICO

CAYMAN ISLANDS

HAITI

JAMAICA

DOMINICAN REPUBLIC

BELIZE

C A R I B B E A N   S E A

HONDURAS

NICARAGUA

PANAMA CANAL

COSTA RICA

VENEZUELA

PANAMA

COLOMBIA

PACIFIC OCEAN

BERMUDA

THE CARIBBEAN

DOMINICAN REPUBLIC

PUERTO RICO

VIRGIN ISLANDS

ANGUILLA

ST. KITTS AND NEVIS

ANTIGUA AND BARBUDA

MONTSERRAT

GUADELOUPE

DOMINICA

ATLANTIC OCEAN

CARIBBEAN SEA

MARTINIQUE

ST. LUCIA

NETHERLANDS ANTILLES

ST. VINCENT AND THE GRENADINES

BARBADOS

GRENADA

TRINIDAD AND TOBAGO

VENEZUELA

GUYANA

SURINAME

FRENCH GUIANA

COLOMBIA

Preface

It gives me great pleasure to introduce this book, which is the product of a great deal of thought by committed Christians not only in the Caribbean but also in North America.

You will notice that it is a book of many voices, some speaking alone, some speaking in concert with others. Of course, those voices have different tones, or personalities, which may be described as academic, or theological, or even ideological.

The documents that we have chosen to include represent statements of significant ecumenical gatherings that have occurred recently in the Caribbean. While the passionate feelings engendered by the various topics of these meetings may have been tempered by the need to speak as one, we think you will agree that the collective voice is powerful, and speaks true.

The Caribbean is a beautiful and complex region. Politically, economically, spiritually, culturally, there is more here than meets the eye. It is more than a playground, but not quite a paradise.

As you read these pages, please try to see what is being described for you. Really listen to these voices, which are authentic and have an important message for the people of North America, and indeed the world.

The book begins with an overview of the history and present reality of the peoples of the Caribbean, by Sergio Arce Martínez and his wife, Dora Valentín, renowned ecumenical leaders in Cuba.

In the first part, "Roots," Dale A. Bisnauth, former associate general secretary of the Caribbean Conference of Churches and now minister of education of Guyana, provides the necessary historical background for an understanding of the present-day situation in the Caribbean.

In the second part we present some of the major issues facing the Caribbean today: poverty and the debt burden, drug traffic, women's rights, and the role of the churches. Adolfo Ham's theological analysis illuminates not only the work of the Caribbean Conference of Churches, but broader matters as well. The interview of Raúl Suárez by Carmelo Alvarez provides a deeply personal and poignant insight into one man's struggle with church and state, social revolution and Christianity, belief and unbelief.

The book ends on a note of hope, which I believe is not misplaced.

New York   OSCAR L. BOLIOLI
November 1992

1

The Caribbean: An Overview

by Sergio Arce Martínez and Dora Valentín

Few countries are less known than those of the Caribbean islands. Yet their importance is anything but small. Like other countries of the Third World, they emerge from a terrible colonialism. They are examples of the originality, the determination, and the creative capabilities of the common people. They are also examples of the tremendous difficulties all Third World countries confront today.

We do well to remember what the Caribbean means in terms of the history of the American hemisphere from the time of Columbus until now. When the first Europeans arrived in the region, those ill-named "discoverers," they began to impose what Cuban patriot José Martí described as "devastating civilization, two words which, antagonistic as they are, nevertheless constitute a whole process." This meant the extermination of the native people and the enslavement of thousands and thousands of women and men torn from the great African continent and brought to America to work in the plantations. These plantations provided a common base from the south of what is now the United States, to the northeastern part of Brazil, by way of the arc formed by the Caribbean islands. Here the sea-going gangsters of every great power fought their horse-thieving quarrels, and their mendacious histories gave them pompous names of wars, admirals, and treaties alike. Here the colonies of more than one old and crumbling empire remained. But here, as well, the Haitian

Sergio Arce Martínez, president of the Christian Peace Movement of Latin America and the Caribbean, was for fifteen years president of the Theological Seminary in Matanzas, Cuba. His wife, Dora Valentín, a civil engineer and a graduate of the theological seminary in Matanzas, is director-general of the Women's Department of the Christian Peace Movement in Cuba. A longer version of this essay was delivered as the keynote speech for the Global Village at Stony Point Center, Stony Point, New York, on July 4, 1992.

Revolution took place, which defeated Napoleon's army, abolished slavery, and opened the door to Latin Americans' independence from European colonialism.

A Common Legacy

The history of the Caribbean Basin since Columbus's arrival is the history of the struggles of empires against our people in order to conquer our lands. However, it is also the story of the struggles of empires among themselves, in order to take over the land conquered by the other. Last, but not least, it is the history of our people to free themselves from any imperialistic master.

Our differences are mainly those of the different metropolises from which our societies originated. Since England was the European country with the most uniform and developed capitalistic growth, its colonialism in the Caribbean was also more developed (that is to say, more implacable, more underdeveloping) even than Spain's. Its colonies were more underdeveloped so that England could grow richer. It is enough to remember the evils of plantation life in the British islands, the so-called West Indies, the cancerous large landholdings (*latifundios*), the parasitic absentee ownership, the overwhelming predominance of slave labor, and the eloquent fact that these nations did not achieve their political independence until as recently as the late 1960s, and not all of them even then.

However, when we say Caribbean, we are talking about one world, similar problems, equal terminology such as colonialism, neocolonialism, *latifundios,* underdevelopment, racism, plantations, slaves, sugar cane, sugar mills, coffee, bananas, slave quarters. It is not just the words we share, but the corresponding cultural complexes as well.

Of course, there are instances where the syncretism does not produce exactly the same results, but they are never very different. Jamaican *potomania* (like Haitian "voodoo") is the equivalent of Cuban *santería*. Does a Cuban or a Dominican, a Puerto Rican or a Haitian need an explanation of Trinidad's calypso? Do not the deeply rooted Cuban *soneros,* Dominican *merengueros,* or Puerto Rican *plenarios* find their counterpart in that country's deep-rooted "calypsonians"? Origins, pains, problems, mixtures, creations, struggles, hopes, religions: above and beyond the futile differences – linguistic and otherwise – we all are joined not only by a common geography, but, more importantly, by a common history.

Something that unites us, culturally speaking, is the anti-colonialistic thought of the literature we have cultivated. This thought, in its refusal to accept the metropolitan impositions, has often energetically reclaimed the pride of our African roots. This undoubtedly contributed to the struggle against colonialism and neocolonialism in the past, as much as in the present. This also has given self-confidence and a sense of dignity to the oppressed and discriminated, even beyond our borders. We make up what Frantz Fanon, another Caribbean writer, called "the people of the Antilles." Haitians and Cubans, Jamaicans and Puerto Ricans, Dominicans and Barbadians, people from Martinique, Guyana, Trinidad and Tobago, Guadeloupe and elsewhere, women and men whose ancestors came or were brought from Africa, Asia, Europe, but who in the final analysis, without disdaining in any way our origin, define ourselves above all by that which we are forging together, by the future we will build in struggle, a future without exploitation, discrimination, misery, illiteracy, colonialism, neocolonialism, hunger . . . in short, without the present international economic system, the cause of all these evils.

The former colonial status of many territories in the Caribbean Basin is reflected in political, social, or cultural dependence, even today. Cuba and other Hispanic ex-colonies have a strong Spanish culture. The French islands together with Guiana have been trans-formed into French overseas departments; the British Caribbean islands have a culture that is predominantly British.

The colonial status was also reflected in our religions. In the former French and Spanish colonies, for example, we find the pre-dominant religion is Roman Catholic. But at the same time, we find Afro-Caribbean cults that are only partially influenced by European religious ideas and that have considerable African elements. People from the low classes who do not adapt so completely to the metropolitan influence are found more attracted to these cults than the members of higher classes. This is important for understanding most of the social, cultural, and political phenomena in the region.

The same is valid in relation to language. Languages are in one way or another, and in different degrees, weapons. They, in our case, are European in a sense and Creole in another. Besides English, French, or Spanish, you will find polyglot languages constituted by words taken, in many cases, from the specific European language and by a linguistic structure that is not European and, in fact, signifies a complete dichotomy between the way of thinking and speaking of many people who live in the same country. Therefore, there exists a complex situation created by the interrelation of two different cultural and social behaviors: on the one hand, the foreign model that has a particular force among the higher classes, and on the other, the Creole culture born in the Caribbean that contains, to a great extent, non-European elements. At first, it may appear that the contradiction between two cultures was a divisive element, not only within each island, but also among the islands and other territories. However, this "contradiction" actually constituted a potential force in the integration of conscience and action that has been initiated during the last twenty-five years.

The Columbus Era

The term "discovery" means primarily "to obtain for the first time something unknown." The lands where Columbus arrived did not constitute "something unknown" for eighty million people and fifteen thousand years of history, individuals who constituted nothing less than one-fifth of the total population of the planet, ten times more than those who inhabited the kingdoms of Spain, from whence the great "discoverers" came.

What really happened in 1492? More than an encounter, more than a confluence or meeting of different cultures or spiritualities. What really happened was rather a clash, a collision: the total crushing of the weaker under the pressure of the stronger in terms of military technique, without any kind of convergence in the political, economical, cultural, or spiritual realms.

To our understanding, in spite of all the tragedy brought about by the demographic catastrophe that destroyed 90 percent of the original American population – in just two generations – and the evident genocide, the most meaningful phenomenon was the violent destruction of their ways of life, of their conceptualization of nature, God, and humankind, the destruction of their political structures, their social manners, private habits, cultural traditions, and religious categories. In the Caribbean this destruction was almost total (99 percent of the population). Only some Caribs survived in two of the smallest islands and two of the continental countries.

The Columbus era began with the destruction of a unique agricultural civilization. Columbus ignited a holocaust of fifty years, but the destruction of the native agricultural system continued afterward by the French, the Dutch, the British, the Portuguese. During the first fifty years of the Columbus era in forty islands, including Cuba, Hispaniola (today Haiti–Dominican Republic), Puerto Rico, and Jamaica, the native population disappeared. In 1492 there were five million inhabitants. Fifty years later only a few thousand remained in the Lesser Antilles.

This original population was well fed. Now, five centuries later, millions of human beings in this area live at the border of starvation. Columbus found in the Caribbean one of the most productive agricultural systems that ever existed. He could not see that more important than gold, pearls, precious stones, and spices were the corn, amaranth, cotton, beans, sweet potatoes, avocados, potatoes, tomatoes, and many other tropical fruits and vegetables.

The pre-Columbus Caribbean was not perfect, but it was reasonably wholesome, with a great deal of complexity, as has been recognized by recent historians. The people had developed a most productive agricultural system, with an adequate amount of water during the dry season assured through well designed irrigation systems. Farming was intensive, and biological control of pests, organic fertilizers, plants able to get nitrogen from air, soil enrichment, crop rotation, and methods of storaging were used. They preserved the forests as a natural resource and tried to keep the living beings they found in those forests. The local people cultivated with scrapers, while the Spaniards introduced the plow pulled by horses or oxen. This new method unbalanced the native agriculture. The plow is efficient only when land is abundant and labor is scarce. It is possible to double production with the hoe, as is being confirmed in Cuba today. As a matter of fact, in Central America it has been proved that the Spanish method of farming reduced the productivity of the soil by 50 percent. Besides the land, the invaders took over the most important natural ecological resource, water, and gave up the place of native farming to the big plantation system.[1]

---

1. See Jan Carew, "Palancas para el cambio: Identidad cultural en el Caribe," *Revista Casa de las Américas* 20, no. 118, 61–69.

A Culture of Resistance

In spite of the conquest and colonization we have suffered, our people at the same time converted themselves into conquerors. A culture of resistance characterizes both Caribbean and Latin American history in general from 1492 until today. This culture of resistance assumed different shapes in its beginning. In many cases, it showed itself as a violent resistance when the natives, practically without any weapons but with audacity and courage, opposed the invaders who stole their lands, their richness, their women. It was the resistance played out in lonely roads, in virgin lands, in forests, in wild mountains, and even in the intimacy of the huts. Persevering, wily, and subversive, this type of resistance was significant for women and even for many children. It is true that the native peoples of the Caribbean practically disappeared, but they bequeathed us their culture of resistance.

The African Negroes, whom the European conquerors and colonizers treated as mere beasts of burden, as subhuman beings, also maintained different degrees of violent resistance. Enslaved Africans greatly outnumbered Europeans in most Caribbean colonies during the eighteenth century, especially in Jamaica, where they organized large-scale uprisings, burned the plantations, and killed the slave masters. Some of the leaders are remembered still, including Cuffy in Guyana, Nanny and Tacky in Jamaica, and Morales in Cuba.[2]

At the end of the eighteenth century (1789), the biggest sugar producer in the Caribbean, Haiti, was the scene of an uprising under the French Revolution slogan, "Liberty, Equality, and Fraternity." The uprising began as a revolt by the free colored (mulattoes) to gain full equality. From a revolt, it escalated into an island-wide slave revolution under the leadership of Toussaint L'Ouverture, a slave. In 1803, after the killing of L'Ouverture by Napoleon's forces, the slaves set up an independent republic.

The Haitian Revolution gave courage to enslaved persons all over the Caribbean. In Guadeloupe and St. Lucia the slaves helped repel British invasion and sustained French revolutionary control. In Grenada and Dominica the slaves joined free mulattoes and resident French. They overthrew the British rebels of the two islands. There was a major slave revolt in Dutch Curaçao.

---

2. See Catherine A. Sunshine, *The Caribbean: Survival, Struggle and Sovereignty* (Washington, D.C.: EPICA, 1985), 12.

If we had a map where we could light a bulb wherever native, slave, and exploited masses revolted in the Caribbean Basin, we would find that since 1492, for five hundred years, there would always be at least one bulb on and most of the time, more than one.[3]

Besides violent resistance, there was a resistance that we can qualify as nonviolent. While some of the native people seemed to accept the invaders, including their culture and manners, their lordship and their religion, in their hearts they did not renounce their identity, culture, or religion. This kind of resistance we can also see in the Africans in a most ostensible way, very important for the Caribbean people.

However, in those ancient years as well as today, certain groups of persons were conquered by "the songs of the mermaid" of the different masters we suffered. They were victims of a particular kind of "cross-eyed" vision of the world. They saw allies where there were only enemies.

The culture of resistance, characteristic of our Caribbean people for over five hundred years, has become today the spiritual factor that opens the possibility of surviving yet another imperialistic onslaught – of overcoming the present war of total extermination waged against the impoverished people of the world by the contemporary international economic order and international political system.

The past has not passed. Past evils have not been destroyed. Conquest and colonization continue. They take more sophisticated forms, but not less cruel and destructive. The foreign debt of the Third World is the most obvious manifestation of the exploitative international system. To this debt we can add another factor, the economic control that the present centers of power (United States, Western Europe, Japan), exert over the impoverished, underdeveloped countries. The exploiter control is carried through the unjust trade relations among nations, the monopoly of the transnational corporations operating upon the strategic sectors of the world economy, the economic policy of the International Monetary Fund and the World Bank prescribed by the money-lender banks and governments, the technological control upon production, the

---

3. See Alejo Carpentier, "La cultura de los pueblos que habitan en las tierras del mar Caribe," *Revista Casa de las Américas,* 20, no. 118, 2-8.

brain-stealing, and the cultural colonization that includes religious penetration.

A Hopeful Spirituality

The five hundredth anniversary of Columbus's arrival concerns us as churchmen and churchwomen. The Catholic as well as the Protestant churches were relevant factors in the process already mentioned. The great majority of their representatives identified themselves mostly with conquerors and colonizers in their depredations and not with their victims. Christianity came to the Caribbean as part of Spanish, French, British, and Dutch colonialism and finally North American neocolonialism. In general, the churches came to assist these powers in building colonial types of societies; they endorsed slavery and helped to entrench racial and class divisions. Something that characterizes most of our nations is that after slavery emancipation and national independence, neither the prophetic role of a few church leaders nor the individual sincerity of many Christians altered this long history of religious collaboration with colonial and neocolonial systems.

In spite of all the weakness of the evangelizing process that we have suffered for five hundred years, the Gospel, in a miraculous way, has helped us in the formation of our culture of resistance. This is something that we share with the rest of Latin America. Only a continent that suffered during these five hundred years the invasion of the Europeans could elaborate a really liberating political theology. Thus we have Latin American "theologies of liberation" and Caribbean "theologies of decolonization." The result of the old evangelization has given us a spiritual unity. Our culture of resistance, a heritage from our native groups and enslaved Africans, has been reinforced by what we call a "hopeful spirituality," a heritage from the Gospel preached, from the Christian faith proclaimed. In spite of the weakness, errors, and evils committed by those who brought us the Christian message of hope and security, we sense that there is a light at the end of the tunnel.

There are signs that point toward the possibility of the realization of our ideals, such as the new movements of African and indigenous Caribbean people; the renewed peasant movements; the ecclesial base communities; the theologies of liberation and decolonization; the many responses to the documents of the fourth conference of

Latin American Roman Catholic bishops in the Dominican Republic in October 1992 (IV CELAM); the Ecumenical Consultation in Jamaica in 1990; the various assemblies and congresses promoted by such ecumenical organizations as the Student Christian Movement and the Christian Peace Movement; the Christian and non-Christian movements promoting the liberation of women and the Christian and non-Christian movements and popular organizations promoting solidarity among the people today, especially with Cuba; various ecumenical organizations involved in serious research about Caribbean problems; some of the activities realized by the Caribbean Conference of Churches (CCC) and the Latin American Council of Churches (CLAI); the four documents approved by the Ecumenical Council of Cuba.

These signs of hope come at a time of a "New International Order" when our region will be subjected to an even higher degree of uncertainty – by the following factors:

(a) The present Caribbean economic stagnation, negative commercial balances, increasing foreign debt, high rate of unemployment, deteriorating life conditions for most of the population and decreasing gross domestic product.

(b) The emergence of new nations in Europe and the consequences in terms of financial assistance, bank credits, preferential trade agreements, and foreign investments.

(c) The marginalization of the Caribbean region before the new commercial megablocs.

(d) The failure of such projects as the Caribbean Basin Initiative promoted by the Reagan administration and other mechanisms for achieving export growth.

(e) The technological changes that generated mainly the substitution of raw materials for synthetic materials.

(f) The threat to the possibility of new investment because of the incapability of offering sophisticated financial services.

These factors, joined with ecological deterioration, a population explosion in many of the islands, and a dynamic informal economic sector, point to the urgent necessity of introducing structural changes in the relationship between the Caribbean and the world economy as well as in the structure of the Caribbean economy itself.

We are going to need now, as never before, our Caribbean culture of resistance and our hopeful spirituality in order to face the risks and threats that the "New International Order" presents us as people and nations.

ROOTS

by Dale A. Bisnauth

Dale A. Bisnauth, a minister of the Guyana Presbyterian Church, is former associate general secretary of the Caribbean Conference of Churches and minister of education in Guyana.

2

Caribbean Profile

Caribbean history did not begin with the arrival of the *Santa María,*
Pinta, and *Niña* in Caribbean waters. Nor should the story of the region's indigenous peoples, the Arawaks and the Caribs, be regarded
as the region's "prehistory."

Just about the time of the dawn of the Christian era, a people
subsequently described as Arawaks left their homes in the Orinoco
basin in South America and migrated northwards. Some of them
settled along the way; many pushed toward the northern waters of
the Caribbean Sea and the Atlantic Ocean. The descendants of those
who reached the northern waters settled on the islands of the Lesser
Antilles. Succeeding generations reached as far north as Hispaniola
and Puerto Rico (around 250 C.E.), Jamaica (around 750 C.E.), Cuba
(around 800 C.E.), and the Bahamas (around 1000 C.E.).

In the wake of the Arawaks came another migrant people, the
Caribs, who probably originated in Brazil, somewhere in the upper
waters of the Amazon River. The Caribs occupied Trinidad for a
while; then their war canoes pushed northward, and they settled in
the islands of the Lesser Antilles as the Arawaks retreated.

Collision of Cultures

On the island where Columbus first landed, which he named San Salvador, the Europeans encountered Arawaks. These aborigines of the
Arawak language group were the gentle Tainos. At that time, Cuba,
the largest of the islands, might have had a population of 100,000,
comprising the Guanajatebeys, an Old Stone Age people, who lived
in the western tip of the island; the Ciboneys, who inhabited the
central part; and the Tainos, who lived in the eastern part of the
island.

The Spanish *conquistadores* made short shrift of the civilization

13

that they found this side of the Atlantic. As luck would have it, it was upon the gentle Arawaks of Hispaniola that the blow of the Spanish Catholics fell first. Not that the Arawaks capitulated meekly, but the reprisals that met their resistance were savage and swift. Even after resistance was quashed in Hispaniola, the *conquistadores* vowed to kill twelve Indians daily in honor of the twelve apostles. A thirteenth was to be immolated in honor of Jesus Christ! Such was the ferocity with which the Spaniards treated the Arawaks that by 1520 their subjugation was complete.

The Caribs of the Lesser Antilles offered stouter resistance to the Spaniards. Ultimately they were spared not because of that resistance, but because the interest of the Europeans had been diverted from the Caribbean to Central and South America where gold and silver had been discovered.

According to the *repartimiento-encomienda* system, established in the Caribbean by 1499, the Spanish Crown gave "commended" Indians to Spanish conquistadors and gentlemen. These *encomenderos* would have the right to exact labor or tribute from the Indians, in return for which they were to provide religious instruction and to offer protection.

Christianization was part of that civilizing process. Martín Fernández de Enciso advanced the theory in 1513 that God had apportioned the Indians to the Spaniards, like the Promised Land for the Jews. In the conquest of Canaan the Israelites slew many Canaanites and enslaved others. According to Fernández de Enciso, this was the will of God because the Canaanites were idolaters.

The theory was accepted by the Spanish Crown. The Crown caused a manifesto or "Requirement" to be announced formally to the Indians before hostilities were launched against them. The *Requerimiento* demanded that the indigenous people acknowledge the Catholic Church as the Ruler and Superior of the whole world. In the name of the pope, the king and queen of Spain were to be acknowledged as superiors, lords, and kings of the Caribbean islands and of the mainland. The Indians were required to allow the Christian faith to be preached to them. If they failed to meet this requirement, they were to be subjugated by force to the Church and the Crown.

Ferdinand and Isabella had wrung extensive concessions from Pope Alexander VI by declaring that their aim in promoting expeditions to the Indies was to extend the dominion of the Roman

Catholic faith. In a series of five papal bulls, the Roman pontiff gave the Spanish Crown the exclusive privilege of Christianizing the Indians; he also gave the Crown such extensive control over the church in the Indies that, for all practical purposes, the king functioned as the pope's vicar in the New World.

By 1502, a Franciscan monastery had been established in Hispaniola; in 1510, the first Dominican monastic center was established when twelve of the "Preaching Brothers" arrived. Special papal bulls permitted the friars to administer the sacraments and to perform other clerical duties if priests were unavailable. The monasteries served as sources of missionaries to new settlements when these were established by *conquistadores* or *encomenderos*.

Challenges to the Spanish Empire

Meanwhile, Spain's monopoly of the Indies, sanctioned by papal bulls and recognized by the Treaty of Tordesillas, was being challenged by its European rivals in the forms of trade, privateering raids, settlement, and conquest.

The first challengers were the Portuguese, who conducted a clandestine trade in African slaves between Guinea in Africa and Hispaniola in the Caribbean. The Portuguese also supplied the Spanish colonists with manufactured European goods. War between France and Spain (1512–58) provided the pretext for French privateers to plunder Spanish shipping and to hold their towns to ransom.

John Hawkins was the first Englishman to infringe on Spain's monopoly of the Caribbean, making his first voyage in 1562 with the purpose of trading illicitly in enslaved Negroes. Hawkins was followed by the more belligerent Francis Drake, whose exploits had the blessing and support of Queen Elizabeth I. By 1573, what amounted to an English privateering war had developed in the Caribbean. Hostilities were brought to an end by the Treaty of London, which was signed in 1604. But, for England, the test of possession (or claim to monopoly) was occupation by English traders and settlers.

Dutch privateering activities in the Caribbean began in 1569 when Dutch and Flemish rebels plundered Spanish shipping as part of the Dutch resistance to Spanish domination of the Netherlands. The Dutch threat to organize a West India Company to promote

Dutch trade in the New World as well as to found colonies there forced Spain to negotiate a truce in 1609.

It was primarily a desire to benefit economically at the expense of Spain that motivated France, England, and the Netherlands to poach on Spain's preserves in the Caribbean. Religious factors were also important in the English and Dutch challenge to Spain's supremacy in the Caribbean. Spain was a Catholic country and the other two were Protestant. When the congregation of Plymouth Church, England, flocked out of the church on the morning of August 9, 1573, to welcome Francis Drake after a voyage to the Indies, it was as much to congratulate a Protestant on his victories against Catholic Spain as it was to welcome an Englishman home.

By treaties in 1559, 1604, and 1609, Spain tacitly accepted the contention that only effective occupation could give it the right to territory beyond the Atlantic. The islands of the Greater Antilles had been occupied by Spanish colonists, but the Lesser Antilles and the Guiana coastlands had not. This encouraged Dutch, English, and French adventurers to attempt to plant colonies in these parts. By 1700, the political map of the Caribbean was vastly different from what it had been a century before, so effectively had Spain's claim to monopoly, based on discovery, been challenged.

The People of the Antilles

The islands "discovered" by Christopher Columbus were called the West Indies (in contrast, apparently, with the East Indies, which Columbus mistakenly thought he had encountered) and included the islands lying between North America and South America. While in the former British colonies "Caribbean" has now replaced "West Indies" for all practical purposes, the old designation persists in such appellations as the West Indian Cricket Team and the West Indian Commission. In the former Dutch colonies, the term "Antilles" has replaced West Indies, and the former French West Indian colonies are now regarded as departments of France. It is no longer fashionable to speak of the former Spanish colonies as the "Indies."

The islands of the Caribbean are grouped into the Greater Antilles and the Lesser Antilles. The Greater Antilles comprises the larger islands of Cuba, Hispaniola (Haiti and the Dominican Republic), Jamaica, and Puerto Rico. The Lesser Antilles is subdivided into the Leeward Islands and the Windward Islands. The smaller "pearls" of the Leewards stretch southeast of Puerto Rico to St. Kitts-Nevis, the Windwards from Guadeloupe to Grenada (excluding Barbados). The Netherlands Antilles comprises Aruba, Bonaire, and Curaçao.

The Caribbean comprises not only the islands strung out "like a necklace of pearls" to Venezuela, but also the Bahamas, Bermuda, and the Turks and Caicos Islands, the South American countries of Guyana, Suriname, and Cayenne (French Guiana), and the Central American country of Belize.

The islands of the Greater, Lesser, and Netherlands Antilles, together with Barbados and Trinidad and Tobago, number twenty-two countries with a population of about 28 million people. When the countries of Belize, Guyana, Suriname, and Cayenne are added, the Caribbean countries number twenty-six, with a population of about 30 million people.

The Language Groups

Thirteen "English-speaking" Caribbean countries make up the trading community known as CARICOM (Caribbean Community and Common Market), along with the United Kingdom dependencies and the United States Virgin Islands.

The CARICOM countries are: Antigua-Barbuda, Bahamas, Barbados, Belize, Dominica, Grenada, Guyana, Jamaica, St. Kitts-Nevis, St. Lucia, St. Vincent, Trinidad and Tobago, and Montserrat. These countries, except Montserrat, became politically independent of Britain after 1960. They are all members of the British Commonwealth of Nations. Montserrat has chosen to remain a colony of Britain.

The other British dependencies are Anguilla, the British Virgin Islands (some fifty small islands forming the northwestern extremity of the Leeward Islands), the Cayman Islands, and the Turks and Caicos Islands.

The United States Virgin Islands include St. Croix, St. Thomas, and St. John. Christiansted, the capital of St. Croix, was once the capital of the Danish West Indies. Its buildings are a reminder of its Danish past. Charlotte Amalie, the capital of St. Thomas, is also the capital of the three United States Virgin Islands.

The Spanish-speaking countries, all one-time colonies of Spain, are Cuba, the largest Caribbean island; Puerto Rico, a United States "commonwealth" and the most easterly of the Greater Antilles; and the Dominican Republic, which, with Haiti, shares the island that Christopher Columbus named Hispaniola.

The Dutch-speaking islands are the "ABC" islands of Aruba, Bonaire, and Curaçao, located near each other, and St. Eustatius, which is a mere eight square miles in size and is part of the Leeward Islands chain. Statia (as St. Eustatius is familiarly called) is still a Dutch colony; so also is the tiny island of Saba. Aruba and Curaçao–Bonaire are independent states. Another Dutch colony is St. Maarten, which shares an island in the Leewards with the French department of St. Martin. To the Dutch-speaking countries must be added the South American country of Suriname, which, in colonial times, was called Dutch Guiana.

The French-speaking countries were so important to France in colonial times that they were considered more valuable than the French territories in North America, including Louisiana. Haiti is French-speaking; but in this, the oldest independent state in the Caribbean, Kreyol (Creole), a popular variant of the French language, is the language of the masses. Martinique, Guadeloupe, and St. Martin of the Leeward Islands are Francophone, and so is Cayenne (French Guiana) on the South American mainland just east of Suriname.

Caribbean Diversity

Caribbean peoples see themselves as Guyanese, Barbadians, Jamaicans, and so on. Intercountry competitions in sports, such as cricket and football, more than anything else, bring out that strong nationalism. However, the region's peoples are capable of transcending nationalistic sentiments when there is a felt need to distinguish between the Caribbean and North America, Europe, or the rest of the world.

It is said with great emphasis at political rallies and elsewhere throughout the Caribbean that "All a we a one" ("All of us are one"). In seemingly culturally divided societies, this is more an expression of hope than a description of reality. Can unity be claimed for a whole region when it seems difficult to establish it even for a single country in that region?

Although Caribbean people live in the same geographical area, for hundreds of years the communication between the countries separated by miles of water has not been good, even when the countries have belonged to the same language group and looked to the same metropolitan center for administrative direction. While it was true that the countries have a common history of plantation dominance and colonial exploitation, there are geographical, economic, ethnic, racial, and cultural differences sufficiently strong to set the Anglophone Caribbean apart from the Dutch-speaking Caribbean and to make the Hispanic Caribbean something of a mystery to the French-speaking Caribbean.

To speak in terms of a common social stratification into two classes – the dominant and the dominated – is simplistic, too, as it ignores the racial divisions in the working class, and indeed in the society as a whole in places like Trinidad, Guyana, and Suriname. Trinidad and Guyana have been described as plural societies, that is, as two or more distinct societies occupying the same geographical space. Perhaps it is more accurate to speak of Caribbean societies rather than of a single Caribbean society.

3

Sugar and Slaves

When the Spaniards discovered that the islands had no gold or silver, attempts were made to cultivate tropical crops and to develop cattle ranches on the larger islands of Hispaniola, Cuba, Jamaica, and Puerto Rico. The idea was to make the Indies profitable for Spain. In this project, the Amerindians, as the conquered people, were expected to supply the required labor.

However, driven to give forced labor over long hours, the Indians died out rapidly. Within two generations after Columbus landed at San Salvador, the Arawaks were practically exterminated. They died from overwork, massacres, and other brutalities at the hands of the conquistadors; they succumbed to European diseases; some committed suicide. On smaller islands such as Grenada, Dominica, and St. Vincent, the Caribs resisted the European intruders, but the outcome was inevitable. Before 1700 in most places, and before 1800 in all, the Amerindians succumbed to the European onslaught.

From 1517 onward, Africans were brought in large numbers to the islands of Hispaniola, Cuba, Jamaica, and Puerto Rico, and to the mainland of Central and South America. The exploitation of both mine and field, it was felt, demanded an abundant labor force inured to tropical conditions. With the rapid depletion of the Indians, Africans were deemed a satisfactory substitute.

With the introduction of sugar into the Caribbean, the islands underwent a dramatic change. Between 1640 and 1655, they were transformed into sugar colonies. Farms gave way to plantations; many small farmers and indentured laborers were ousted to make room for African slaves. When Jamaica was acquired by the English and St. Domingue by the French, they too became sugar colonies. But the English began their own slave trade, which lasted from 1651 to 1808; that trade introduced an estimated 1,900,000 million Africans into the Caribbean. The French trade in slaves lasted from

1664 to 1830; it brought some 1,650,000 blacks to the region. Meanwhile, the Dutch brought another 200,000 to the Guianas, Curaçao, Aruba, Bonaire, and St. Eustatius.

With the development of the sugar plantations, it seemed as if the colonies would at last realize their potential of becoming prosperous. "The jewel in England's crown" was the description given to the British West Indian colonies in the eighteenth century. Sugar brought huge profits to the European "owners" of the sugar colonies, and as the European nations went to war to defend their possessions and their profits, many small islands changed ownership several times.

A Troubled Society

But eighteenth-century Caribbean society was an unhappy society. On every plantation, in every colony, the enslaved blacks far outnumbered the white members of the plantocracy. Members of the plantocracy lived in constant fear of rebellion and resistance, so the owners and managers of estates were repressive in their treatment of the blacks. In the French and Spanish Caribbean, codes of slave law existed to regulate the treatment of slaves. Officers were appointed to ensure that the slave laws were enforced, but these regulations were violated with impunity. The Dutch, too, had an official to ensure that slaves were not mistreated, but he could always be persuaded to turn a blind eye when slaves were punished. The English legislated no slave code. Each English island had a local assembly that made laws. However, comprising as it did members of the plantocracy, such an assembly could not be expected to restrict the powers of slave-owners.

Most slaves spent their lives in a continuous round of hard, enforced labor. This routine was interrupted only by the Sunday morning visit to the market where they traded in vegetables, fruits, and other small produce, which they raised on their provision grounds.

The achievement of legal freedom was extremely difficult but not impossible for an enslaved person in the Caribbean. It depended on the "generosity" of slave-holders. A runaway was severely punished, if caught, but Africans did run away, particularly in those countries where they could hide easily. The "Bush Negroes" of Dutch Guiana escaped to the upper reaches of rivers where rapids made it dangerous to chase after them. The "Maroons" of Jamaica escaped from the Spanish during the British capture of the island and settled in inaccessible mountain country from which they conducted raids on nearby plantations. Dominica, St. Vincent, and St. Lucia also had Maroon communities in the mountains.

But there was another phenomenon that led to "freedom." In the late eighteenth century, from 5 to 25 percent of the population of Caribbean countries consisted of free colored people. These were the offspring of white fathers (members or employees of the plantocracy) and African slave mothers. Interracial sexual liaisons, though criticized by visitors to the Caribbean, were openly countenanced in those islands where white women were few. White men in some societies not only recognized their mixed offspring but also educated them in Europe and left them substantial properties. Some colored families rose to prominence and even rivaled whites in wealth and style of life.

The slave revolt so long dreaded by the plantocracy occurred in the French colony of St. Domingue (Haiti) in 1791–92. It was occasioned by the outbreak of the French Revolution of 1789. The free colored in St. Domingue demanded the right to vote from the National Assembly in Paris in 1791; they obtained it, much to the chagrin of the whites. When the whites of St. Domingue refused to recognize the decree of the National Assembly, the mulattoes rose in insurrection. Both whites and mulattoes were caught by surprise when a slave rebellion broke out in August in the north of the island. The struggle for liberation lasted for several years despite efforts from the British and the Spanish to quell it, ostensibly to rescue the white population but actually as part of a general attack on France in the course of which Britain hoped to annex St. Domingue. The expulsion of the British was effected by Toussaint L'Ouverture, the leader of the slave revolt.

The revolt of St. Domingue was not the first uprising in the Caribbean. In 1763, there was an uprising in Berbice, Guiana, against the Dutch. It was put down fairly early. Other uprisings occurred in places like Jamaica, Barbados, and British Guiana. None was as successful as the St. Domingue revolt, but all focused attention on the conditions under which people lived and worked and from which they desired to be freed. The revolts represented the Africans' contribution to the eventual abolition of the institution of slavery.

The End of Slavery

The abolition of the slave trade and the emancipation of slaves in the British West Indies were brought about not only by agitation in Britain against the inhumanity of slavery but also by the protests there that an economy based on slave labor and dependent on British mercantilist trade policies was against the best interests of Britain. Abolition and emancipation were effected by legislation passed in the House of Commons in England in 1807.

But while the British trade came to an end in 1807 and the French trade in the 1830s, Spain and Portugal continued to develop their colonies with enslaved people. The Americans shipped slaves both for themselves and for the Spanish and Portuguese territories, particularly Cuba and Brazil, until the issue of slavery was taken to the point of civil war in the United States in 1861.

It took another twenty-five years for slavery to end in the Caribbean. In the Danish Virgin Islands, general emancipation came to St. Thomas and to St. John after those islands were rocked by slave revolts. The slaves of the French islands of Martinique and Guadeloupe were freed by the French Revolution only to be re-enslaved a decade later; they were finally emancipated in 1848. In the British West Indies, full emancipation came in 1838. The slaves of St. Maarten were in effect free after 1848 when they moved from the Dutch to the French half of the island. In Curaçao and Bonaire, an amelioration edict, passed in 1857, proved to be as unsatisfactory to masters as it was to slaves, and emancipation was granted in the Dutch islands as it was in Suriname in 1862, although freedom was delayed until 1873. It was not until 1886, however, that the Spanish government freed the slaves of Cuba.

Notions related to "the rights of man" no doubt helped to inspire the revolution that led to the freedom of about 450,000 persons in St. Domingue (Haiti). Similarly, the anti-slavery movement in Britain that led to freedom for about 650,000 persons in the British Caribbean must have been inspired by the evangelical fervor of the members and supporters of the Society for the Abolition of Slavery. Reformist ideas prevalent in Europe might have led the French, Dutch, and Spanish governments to free people who had been enslaved in the French and Dutch Antilles and the Spanish Indies of Cuba, Puerto Rico, and Santo Domingo. But emancipation became a possibility only when economic self-interest coincided with social morality.

This was clearly demonstrated in the case of the British West Indian countries. The wealth from the sugar islands helped to bring about the British Industrial Revolution, but that revolution then made the West Indian sugar monopoly a hindrance to free enterprise. When British Caribbean planters competed in markets glutted by cheaper sugar from St. Domingue, Brazil, and Cuba, and later from beet sugar, only monopoly prices enabled them to survive. Moreover, British industrial interests chafed over the restrictions that confined trade to British West Indian islands that could absorb only a fraction of British manufactured goods. The abolition of the slave trade and the emancipation of slaves were meant, in part at least, to weaken the West Indian sugar interest and to break the monopoly of trade. Significantly, many people who helped bring about emancipation in the British islands supported slavery in Brazil, Cuba, and the southern region of the United States, where free trade made it possible for British manufacturers to obtain cheap raw material.

Imported Workers

Sugar interests in the Caribbean stuck to the production of their staple. Planters argued that the very survival of West Indian society depended on the survival of the sugar plantation. It was argued that without sugar and the white plantocracy, the freed Negroes would lapse into barbarism. Haiti was held up as the example of a degenerate country. But sugar cultivation demanded a large manipulable labor force and the freed Africans were not amenable to constituting that force, not even for the wages that they were now paid. Planters used every constraint to force the ex-slaves to remain on the estates and to work on them. But the effectiveness of the constraints depended on the alternatives available to the blacks. On small, densely populated islands such as Barbados, Antigua, and St. Kitts, where plantations absorbed all the cultivable land, ex-slaves had little choice but to remain on and work for plantations. Where land was available, as in Jamaica, Trinidad, Cuba, Puerto Rico, and British Guiana, ex-slaves either bought or squatted on such lands and occupied themselves in cash-crop farming.

In order to ensure themselves a steady, large, and manipulable labor force and to depress wages where some ex-slave wage-labor was available, planters resorted to the importation of indentured immigrant labor. In this effort, they received the support and assistance of governments. After 1840, hundreds of thousands of indentured immigrants came to the Caribbean to take the place of the slaves on the plantations and, in some cases, to work alongside ex-slaves in the production of sugar.

Madeirans (Portuguese) began to come regularly from around 1840, primarily to British Guiana. Chinese immigration to Trinidad and British Guiana was sustained from 1859 to 1866; between 1852 and 1874, Cuba imported some 125,000 Chinese laborers from Amoy and Canton. Attempts to induce Africans of Sierra Leone and the Kru Coast to migrate to the West Indies were not so successful, but by the end of the 1860s a total of 36,160 free Africans had been brought to such places as British Guiana, Jamaica, Trinidad and St. Kitts.

Chinese and Madeirans suffered heavy mortality. Many of those who survived left sugar cultivation to take up peddling and retail shopkeeping. This caused the planters of Trinidad, British Guiana, and Suriname, in particular, to turn to India for their labor supply. By the time the Indian government suspended indentureship, Indians had come to the Caribbean in the numbers shown in the table below. When their contracts expired, most of these Indian indentured laborers chose to remain in the Caribbean.

Indian Immigration to the Caribbean	
British Guiana	239,000
Trinidad	134,000
Suriname	35,000
Jamaica	33,000
St. Lucia	4,000
Grenada	3,000
St. Vincent	2,700
St. Kitts	300
Guadeloupe/ Martinique	78,000
French Guiana	19,000

Toward Self-Government

While the arrival of Madeirans, Chinese, and Indians was changing the demographic map of the Caribbean, in the British Caribbean the possibility of colored and black persons qualifying for the franchise and for seats in the local legislatures forced the plantocracy to accept a regression from the self-government to which they were accustomed to British Colonial Office rule.

In Jamaica, Crown Colony government replaced that of a representative assembly after the Morant Bay uprising of 1865 in which many persons were killed by the local militia during the protest demonstrations against poverty and injustice. During the last third of the nineteenth century all the British countries except Barbados came under Crown Colony government. Many blacks and coloreds welcomed Crown Colony government at that time, since they felt that without the protection of Her Majesty's Government, their fellow colonists (i.e., the whites) would oppress them. And while some English colonists favored Crown rule as a protection of blacks and coloreds against local white oligarchies, others welcomed it as an effective way of preventing blacks from coming into political power on the strength of their numbers. In the end, government by the Colonial Office turned out to be government by the Caribbean mercantile class. Its programs of reform were skewed in favor of the white elite and, later, of the colored middle class.

Crown Colony government in the British territories survived intact until the 1930s when the worldwide economic depression began to cause unrest in the Caribbean as it did elsewhere in the world. Strikes and riots broke out in every country from Jamaica in the north to British Guiana in the south. These acts of violence and unrest were as much against Crown Colony government, which made it impossible for Caribbean people to redress their own hardships, as against low wages and poor living conditions.

Important changes were made in the Jamaican government in 1944, and in the early 1950s other British colonies took steps toward self-government, the first of which was universal adult suffrage.

Similar changes were taking place in the French, Dutch, and U.S. colonies, where the inhabitants were given a greater share in the governance of their own affairs, but not political independence. A nationalist movement began in Puerto Rico, but unrest in 1937 resulted in the Ponce Massacre in which Puerto Rican students were killed, much to the shock of the American public. The move for independence lost much of its momentum when the Little New Deal program was launched to address the deplorable social and economic conditions on the island and when a Puerto Rican party was formed to undertake that program for economic progress.

In the period before World War II some attempts had been made by Caribbean peoples to foster cooperation among several British colonies. Cooperation was hindered by poor communication over long stretches of water, by the insularity that isolation breeds, and by the fact that several countries were competitors in the same overseas markets. Jamaicans found it quicker to communicate with Halifax than with Trinidad, and Barbadians found it easier to reach New York by mail than British Guiana in days when mail between Trinidad, Jamaica, Barbados, and Guiana usually passed through either London, New York, or Halifax.

After World War II there was a new openness to the idea of a West Indian federation. Such a body came into existence in April 1958, but by 1962 it was dissolved. Some of the old distrust bred by insularity was no doubt responsible for the breakup of the federation. But other factors were responsible as well, namely, the desire of island politicians for national independence.

No sooner had the federation dissolved than Jamaica and Trinidad and Tobago became independent states. Barbados was to follow, and Guyana in 1966. But political independence was not matched by economic viability. The struggle since political independence has been after that viability as well as cultural integrity.

4

Under the Eagle

By the time of the U.S. Civil War (1861–65), the United States had all but achieved what some Americans believed was that nation's "Manifest Destiny" by filling in the map from the Atlantic to the Pacific and from Canada to the Gulf of Mexico and the Rio Grande River.

Already some had begun to cast a longing eye on Cuba, the largest of the Caribbean islands and, at that time, a rich Spanish colony. Offers to buy the island (the most generous by James Polk) were rebuffed by Spain. But interest in the island continued, particularly since U.S. investors had developed plantations for growing sugar and other products.

Spanish-American War

A revolt against Spain broke out in Cuba in 1895. U.S. sentiment, whipped to a high pitch by the sensational newspapers of William Randolph Hearst and Joseph Pulitzer, strongly supported the Cubans, but the United States refrained from entering the civil war. However, on February 15, 1898, the U.S. battleship *Maine* exploded mysteriously in Havana Harbor, killing some 260 Americans. Spain denied any involvement in the incident. Nevertheless, urged by the public and the press under the slogan "Remember the Maine," the McKinley administration declared war on Spain, ostensibly to free Cuba from Spain while leaving the government and control of the island to its people.

At the end of the Spanish-American War, the United States had become a world power. Spain ceded Puerto Rico and the Philippines to the United States. Cuba was not annexed, but in 1902, when a constitution for an independent Cuba went into effect, it contained the Platt Amendment. Passed in the U.S. Congress in

1901, that amendment awarded the U.S. government the right to naval bases on the island and the right to intervene in the internal affairs of Cuba in order to preserve Cuban independence and to maintain order. For all practical purposes, Cuba became a protectorate of the United States.

Down to about 1900 or so, U.S. leaders rejected the notion of acquiring colonies in the Caribbean in the traditional sense. But the United States did not reject the notion of extending hegemony over the region. At times, the United States would exercise that imperialism for self-serving interests; at other times, it would plead a good-faith effort to impose its notions of political order, economic stability and growth, and civic morality on this or that country.

A number of factors — some strategic, some economic — helped to determine the role the United States would play in the region. Its modern navy needed bases. In 1900, Admiral George Dewey, the commander of the Pacific fleet in the Spanish-American War, recommended the acquisition of naval bases in Cuba, the development of a base at Culebra in Puerto Rico, and the seizure of base sites in the Dominican Republic and Haiti. People like Andrew Carnegie and David Wells were expounding their "glut theory" to explain a perceived crisis in the U.S. economy and to suggest that the future of U.S. capitalism demanded an aggressive export expansion to new markets. New markets, according to those who saw economic expansion as the cure of the malaise in the U.S. economy, were to be found in East Asia, Latin America, and the Caribbean.

The "glut theory" of Carnegie and Wells added a new dimension to U.S. foreign policy: it integrated the search for foreign markets with U.S. strategic considerations. Meanwhile, Benjamin Kidd was advocating that a dedicated cadre of trained, God-fearing civil servants be dispatched from the civilized and civilizing nations to train people in the tropics in the art of civilization and civil government. Many Americans who read Kidd accepted his premise about the white man's duty to the people of the tropics. Much in the vein of Benjamin Kidd, William McKinley declared that the United States had an obligation to the "uncivilized peoples" of those countries once occupied by Spain to raise their political, economic, and moral levels.

Monroe Doctrine

Theodore Roosevelt, who became president of the United States on the death of William McKinley, believed that the Caribbean countries could develop, however defective their social and political systems were at that time. While that improvement was taking place, however, it was imperative that European nations be discouraged from encroaching into the strategically important Caribbean world. The Monroe Doctrine could be invoked to keep out the Europeans.

Developed from a statement that President James Monroe made to Congress in 1823 relative to European–Latin American relationships, the doctrine assumed the status of a foreign policy principle. It stipulated that (a) European nations must not try to impose their system of government upon the New World; if they did, the United States would consider it sufficient reason for declaring war against them; (b) the United States would respect existing European colonies in the Western hemisphere; (c) no new colonies should be formed in the Western hemisphere; and (d) the United States would not interfere in the internal affairs of Europe.

Roosevelt's own corollary to that doctrine could be invoked to justify intervention in any country in the hemisphere. That corollary ran:

> Chronic wrong-doing, or an impotence which results in a general loosening of the ties of civilized society, may in America as elsewhere ultimately require intervention by some civilized nation, and in the Western Hemisphere the adherence of the United States to the Monroe Doctrine may force the United States, however reluctantly, in flagrant cases of such wrong-doing or impotence, to the exercise of an international power.

The U.S. presence was not without its benefits. There was, generally, an improvement in roads, medical services, public health and sanitation measures, and other infrastructural systems. But it is doubtful whether the United States succeeded in instilling democratic virtues in its client states. A small elite committed to the U.S. and what was perceived as the American way of life developed and grew wealthy, while the bulk of the population remained impoverished. While U.S. business, trade, and investment flourished, a strong and vitriolic anti-Americanism flourished as well, particularly in Cuba, where U.S. materialism was soon in evidence. Americans, in turn, became contemptuous and cynical of Caribbean politics and politicians, economics, and culture.

Before World War II, the United States relinquished the Platt Amendment, which had made Cuba a protectorate and which was a source of annoyance to younger Cubans. However, Sumner Welles, the U.S. ambassador extra-ordinary and plenipotentiary, carefully supervised the rise of Fulgencio Batista to power. Batista guaranteed internal political stability and close cooperation with the United States. Cuba was assured of a sugar quota to the States, which in return demanded preferences for its products in the Cuban economy. Meanwhile, the United States "ruled" Haiti through compliant Haitians mainly of the elite class. Americans, as well as the elite, felt that the Haitian blacks were ignorant and incapable of self-rule. Blacks grew to resent the Americans, while the latter resented being resented.

In the Dominican Republic, internecine quarrels after 1922 among self-serving Dominican opportunists caused the Americans to tolerate Rafael Trujillo as dictator with the hope that he would establish lasting peace in that country.

Puerto Rico, which had been described by Americans as "our vest-pocket republic," was by the Organic Act of 1900 granted a government (after U.S. military rule) of one house elected by universal male suffrage. The country was effectively ruled, though, by an American governor and a team of civil servants in an executive council with five other persons, all appointed by the president of the United States and answerable to him.

World War II

World War II brought the Caribbean closer to the United States. During the war, the U.S. dispatched military missions and economic advisors to the region. Busy centers developed to service U.S. installations and bases. The United States purchased Caribbean agricultural and mineral products and became the major source of manufactured goods for the region. (European markets had been disrupted and the flow of trade between Europe and the Caribbean had practically ceased because of the fear of German submarine activities in the Atlantic.)

Five days after Pearl Harbor, the Caribbean was designated an American Coastal Frontier. It was as obvious to Caribbean people as to Americans that in the event of a German naval, submarine, or air strike, the United States would have to defend the region. To Americans, the prospect that Hitler might compel the defeated Western European nations to cede their Caribbean possessions to Germany seemed a real and frightening possibility. In 1940, there-fore, Congress expressed its determination not to recognize the transfer of New World territory from one non-American power · to another. Cordell Hull, the U.S. secretary of state, affirmed the Monroe Doctrine as a statement of self-defense.

During the war itself, in Trinidad, where there was a U.S. base, animosity flared between white soldiers and black Trinidadians. But by the end of the war, Trinidadian calypsonians were singing "An Ode to America, the veteran champion of democracy." (The "Rum and Coca-Cola" calypso also described the rise in prostitution that had resulted from the presence of so many U.S. soldiers on the is-land.) By the end of World War II, the Caribbean had become so closely tied to the U.S. that more than ever it could be described as a U.S. *mare clausam,* a kind of American Mediterranean.

Cold War Alignments

The end of the armed conflict saw the beginning of the U.S. Cold War with its wartime ally, the Soviet Union. By that time, the United States was the number one military and economic power in the world. Its industries had grown rapidly and immensely during the war years, and it had suffered no infrastructural damage.

At the Bretton Woods economic conference in 1944, the dollar was established as the standard by which all other currencies, in-cluding gold, would be measured. The World Bank was set up to facilitate the reconstruction of the Western world, much of which was ravaged by World War II; so also was the International Monetary Fund, which would regulate (and control) all Western economies according to U.S. criteria and on U.S. terms.

President Truman perceived the Soviet Union as the great poten-tial enemy to be contained. From 1945, any resistance by peoples against what they perceived to be oppressive governments would be seen by the United States as part of a Russian plot to impose communism on the world. The United States felt compelled to support those governments that resisted movements for radical change as a counter to alleged Russian ambitions. In 1947, the Truman administration set up the Central Intelligence Agency (CIA) to handle overseas security threats to U.S. interests. "Threats" were generally interpreted to mean threats of communism.

Naturally, the United States wanted its own Western hemisphere to be orderly, loyal to its Cold War policies, and not too demanding in terms of economic assistance, since resources were needed at home and in Europe for reconstruction and revitalization of world capitalism. That revitalization was seen as necessary to restrict the spread of communism.

In the Caribbean, political leaders who were clamorously anticommunist easily attracted the support of the United States. In Haiti, where years of U.S. "rule" had not resulted in any significant measure of prosperity for the Haitian people and where politics were dominated by confrontation between a mulatto elite and a new generation of politically aware blacks, the Americans supported Paul Magloire, a mulatto military officer. Magloire was loud in his declamation against communism and quick in his promise to fight that evil to the death. When François Duvalier became president of Haiti in 1956, he pursued both U.S. aid and an anti-communist stance.

Rafael Trujillo of the Dominican Republic posed as the anticommunist *par excellence* and thus assured himself of U.S. support to keep himself in power – even though the U.S. ambassador, Ellis Briggs, described him in 1944 as a dictator who was opposed to fundamental democratic principles. Trujillo employed lobbyists and public relations specialists on Capitol Hill to guard his image and the Dominican Republic's sugar quota. The Senate was convinced that because elections were held periodically, Trujillo could not be a dictator. In any case, the feeling was that the United States should not interfere in the internal affairs of the republic. At least, not yet.

No More Cubas

Fulgencio Batista of Cuba seized power in 1952 and got away with it because of his anti-communist stance and his image as the valiant strongman capable of maintaining order and promoting U.S.-style progress in Cuba. Arthur Gardner, U.S. ambassador to Cuba during the Eisenhower administration, was loud in his praise of Batista, while the Cuban nightlife dazzled visitors. It seemed that the island had become a lucrative marketplace.

Meanwhile, the most dramatic political event in twentieth-century Caribbean history was taking shape. In 1953, Fidel Castro Ruz began his struggle to restore constitutional government in Cuba and to replace the Batista dictatorship. He declared his cause as nationalistic, anti-imperialistic, and anti-colonialist. He was careful to indicate that he had no hatred for the American people. But Castro combined the strong anti-American sentiment of the Cuban people, who for a long time had resented the U.S. role in their country's political life, with the socialism that had had a long history among Cuban intellectuals, to provide his cause with the inspiration that eventually led to the success of the Cuban Revolution.

But the United States demanded – and got – the expulsion of Cuba from the Organization of American States. Cuba then turned to the Soviet Union, as it feared another U.S. invasion. On May Day, 1962, Russia declared Cuba an ally and began to support that country economically. Russia also helped to boost Cuba's military supplies. The installation of Russian missiles on the island created a serious crisis in 1962.

Also in the early 1960s, the U.S. government, convinced that economic strangulation would ruin Cuba and bring about the destruction of Castro, imposed an economic blockade on Cuba, which became hemispheric policy. But the Cuban Revolution survived, and this small Caribbean nation has so far successfully challenged U.S. hegemony in this hemisphere.

The success of Cuba has undoubtedly been an inspiration to left-oriented politicians in the Caribbean and in Central America. But, in a real sense, that success has also been the principal reason why left-oriented political leaders and parties have not been allowed to come to office, however popular they might be; or, if they came to office, they have not been allowed to stay in power for long. Preventing another Cuba from emerging became the overriding goal of the United States for the Caribbean up to the end of the Cold War.

The U.S. *Mare Clausum*

It was almost an open secret that the Anglophone Caribbean countries were exchanging one imperial master for another. The United States was moving into the place once occupied by Britain in much the same way that it had moved into those islands that were once under Spanish governance and influence.

Jamaica became independent in 1962; Trinidad and Tobago became independent that same year. U.S. products began to replace British manufactured goods on the shelves of stores and supermarkets, and multinational companies like Texaco, Reynolds, and Alcoa were beginning to move in, eyeing Trinidad's oil and Jamaica's and British Guiana's bauxite.

It would not be long before U.S. cultural influences would begin to penetrate the region in earnest – especially in the English-speaking islands. Already, American films were becoming as popular as Coca-Cola, and rock-'n'-roll music and American "pop" songs competed successfully with calypso and *ska* on Caribbean radio. it would not be long also before a new wave of U.S.-based religious movements would sweep through the region and penetrate as far south as Guyana as the radio brought Billy Graham and the Lutheran Brotherhood Hour with Richard DeHaan into people's living rooms.

Meanwhile, the political leadership of Jamaica was quick to identify Jamaica's destiny with the United States. Alexander Bustamante, the first minister of independent Jamaica, declared that the United States could establish a military base on that island without committing itself to make aid available to the newly independent country. Dr. Eric Williams, first prime minister of independent Trinidad and Tobago and eminent authority on West Indian history, opted to develop Trinidad and Tobago on the Puerto Rican model.

Overt interference occurred in October 1983, during Ronald Reagan's administration, when U.S. troops landed in Grenada. The justification for what the Reagan administration described as an "intervention" was the protection of U.S. citizens jeopardized by violence after Prime Minister Maurice Bishop and some of his colleagues were assassinated by members of Bishop's political party, the New Jewel Movement.

Caribbean reaction to the intervention was mixed. Some leaders applauded it as necessary because of the acts of terrorism that had been perpetrated on the island; others condemned it as an invasion by the superpower that had resented Grenada's close friendship with Cuba and had used the violence as a pretext. The landing of some six thousand Marines in Grenada underscored the fact that the United States would not tolerate challenges to its hegemony in the region.

5

Religious Crossroads

Missionaries and Indians

From the beginning of the Conquest missionaries accompanied the conquistadors. The Cross and the Crown generally worked in tandem in the task of "civilizing" the Indians, but there were significant exceptions. As he stood in the pulpit of his church in Santo Domingo and faced the wealthiest and most influential colonists in Hispaniola, Antonio de Montesinos asked his congregation on the Sunday before Christmas in 1511:

> Tell me, by what right and justice do you keep these Indians in such cruel and humble servitude? Why do you keep them so oppressed and weary, not giving them enough to eat, not taking care of them in their illness? For with the excessive work you demand of them, they fall ill and die, or rather you kill them with your desire to extract and acquire gold every day. Are these not men? Are you not bound to love them as you love yourselves?

Bartolomé de Las Casas had taken part in the conquest of Cuba and had been an *encomendero* there. He did not agree with Montesinos that it was evil to enslave the Indians and was present when some of the worst atrocities were committed against the Indians of Cuba. While he was preparing his Whitsuntide sermon in 1514, however, he had a change of heart. He was struck by the text: "He that sacrificeth of a thing wrongly gotten, his offering is ridiculous and the gifts of unjust men are not accepted." From that time on, Las Casas became an indefatigable champion of the Indian cause. He freed his own Indians and went to Spain to lobby both the Crown and the hierarchy of the church on behalf of the indigenous people. He was appointed Protector of the Indians and sent to Hispaniola to supervise a commission of friars investigating whether or not Indians were fit to be free.

Las Casas soon discovered that protecting the indigenous people was an impossible task. The Spanish settlers were not prepared to give up their labor force, which they felt was indispensable for the exploitation of mine, farm, or ranch; they were not ready to teach the Amerindians the virtues of Christianity. The Indians were not prepared to abandon their way of life, nor to convert to belief in the God of the Catholic Spaniards.

In 1517, Las Casas and a number of ecclesiastics addressed a memorial to the Spanish Crown outlining how the development of Spanish-Indian communities in the New World might proceed. The memorial suggested that Negroes might be better employed in the place of Indian labor because the Negro was sturdier and better equipped to undertake the heavy work demanded by the Spanish settlers. Las Casas, who became bishop of Chiapas in 1544, later regretted having made the suggestion, deeming it as unjust to enslave Negroes as it was to enslave Indians, but he has not been forgiven by Caribbean blacks for having made that suggestion.

Whatever the weaknesses of the Spanish Catholic mission to the indigenous peoples, the Spanish Catholics at least made an attempt to incorporate these peoples within the fold of the church. With the Dutch who settled on the South American mainland in what later came to be called the Guianas, it was different. The Dutch Reformed Church and the Dutch Lutheran Church served as chaplaincies to the Dutch planters. They had no mission to the indigenous peoples. Later, when the Dutch employed slave labor, they did not even think of introducing Christianity to the natives of Africa.

The British who settled in the Caribbean were mainly members of the Church of England. The Rev. John Featly, probably the first Anglican cleric to minister in the Caribbean, accompanied the first settlers to St. Kitts. In a sermon based on Joshua 1:8, preached at St. Botolph's, Aldersgate, just before Thomas Warner's company departed for the West Indies, Featly likened the settlers to seventeenth-century "Israelites" about to break into the strongholds of heathen unbelievers, or like crusaders about to wrest lands from infidels. Whether it was the inspiration of their religion or their need for safety (or both) that motivated them in 1625, the English in St. Kitts, with the help of the Huguenot settlers under Pierre Belain d'Esnambuc, surprised the Caribs and massacred them. Even Chief

Tegremond, without whose goodwill and assistance the settlement could not have been founded, was killed.

A Gospel of Submission

In the same vein, later Protestant missionaries for the most part did little to challenge the institution of slavery. One might expect that missionaries who had recognized the humanity of blacks enough to work for the salvation of their souls and whose work was primarily among enslaved persons would support the movements for abolition, amelioration, and emancipation that which so crucially affected the welfare of their converts. The truth is that one looks in vain for a positive, uncompromising declaration of the part of the evangelical missionaries in the Caribbean against the institution of slavery. Whatever their personal views on slavery, the missionaries were hesitant to make those views public.

Count Nicholas Ludwig von Zinzendorf, an influential Moravian pietist and dominant figure at the Herrnhut community in Saxony, sent the first evangelical missionaries to the Danish islands of the Caribbean in 1732. Zinzendorf had in fact seen nothing wrong with slavery. On February 15, 1739, the count advised the slave converts in St. Thomas:

> Be true to your husbands and wives, and obedient to your masters.... The Lord has made all ranks – kings, masters, servants and slaves. God has punished the first Negroes by making them slaves, and your conversion will make you free, not from the control of your masters, but simply from your wicked habits and thoughts and all that makes you dissatisfied with your lot.

The Moravian Church's acceptance of the status quo, advocacy that slaves also accept it because it was of divine ordering, and emphasis on industry on the part of slave children were calculated to entrench slavery. In fact, Moravian missionaries operated New Carmel, an estate in Jamaica that came into their possession around 1754, by the use of slave labor, thus demonstrating that they saw nothing incompatible between Christianity and slavery. Little wonder that planters invited Moravian missionaries to evangelize their Negro slaves.

As the campaign for the abolition of the slave trade gained momentum in Britain, the evangelical clergymen in the Caribbean came under suspicion of the plantocracy. This was particularly the case with the Methodists since it was known that John Wesley was opposed to slavery. In Jamaica in 1790, the Methodist evening service was discontinued on the charge by the Guard Jury of Kingston that it was unsettling to the general peace and quiet of the inhabitants. The St. Domingue revolt (1791–93) made the whites of the Caribbean fearful for their lives and safety. The assembly of St. Vincent passed an act forbidding missionaries to preach to slaves. Matthew Lumb disregarded the legislation and was jailed. Robert Gamble was so badly beaten on the instigation of planters that he died from his injuries.

Evangelical missionaries were persecuted not because they actually advocated the abolition of the slave trade, but because they were suspected of being in sympathy with the cause advocated by some of their co-religionists in England. And, after all, the bulk of the membership of their chapels and meeting-houses consisted of blacks. But the evangelical missionaries all observed the instructions given to them on their arrival in the colonies – to pursue their sole business of promoting the moral and religious improvement of the slaves without interfering with the institution of slavery. They were not to engage in disputes over civil matters or matters related to local policies either orally or by correspondence with persons in England or in the colonies.

On August 1, 1834, the Emancipation Act was passed by the British Parliament. The evangelicals in the Caribbean, unlike their counterparts in Britain, could claim little credit for that momentous legislation. Neither could the Church of England in the Caribbean.

Christianity and Social Status

Emancipation was followed by a heightening of missionary activity in the British Caribbean, which had an interesting effect on Caribbean society. To be Christian became an important criterion of social worth. The fact that important people in the society were Christians – including government officials, school teachers, and ministers of religion – helped to strengthen that feeling.

Meanwhile, in the schools of the British Caribbean that operated under the patronage of the churches and were staffed by persons appointed by the churches, the importance of English cultural values was stressed. Those values were inculcated in the coloreds and Negroes who were educated in the schools and became part of their criteria of personal worth and excellence. By the end of the nineteenth century, a "greater tradition" of cultural values had developed in the British West Indies.

Way into the twentieth century, Caribbean society remained segmented. But a social consensus had developed around such values as an education in English, adherence to the Christian religion, the ability to speak English correctly, the identification of the self with the superior British race, and the possession of a light or fair complexion.

Given the above, one would expect the Church of England to prove attractive to British Caribbean peoples. It did. Between 1871 and 1890 – the heyday of British colonial expansionism – the membership of the Anglican Church in Jamaica alone jumped from 19,576 to 40,298. Between 1874 and 1880, William Piercy Austin, the bishop of Guiana, was averaging a thousand confirmations a year. Elsewhere in the Caribbean, the growth of the Church of England was steady. In comparison to the Anglican Church, the growth of Methodism was solid but not spectacular. It was not long before the Church of England was outstripping, in membership growth, the Moravians, Methodists, and Congregationalists who were evangelizing among the Negroes long before the Anglicans began to take an interest in them. Undoubtedly, the fact that the Church of England was the established church and the church of the governing classes in the British colonies made membership in that church desirable. Not a few persons who were once Congregationalists, Moravians, Methodists, or Baptists became Anglicans, particularly in Barbados, Jamaica, and the Bahamas. As people acquired an education good enough to aspire to positions in the teaching profession and in the lower echelons of civil service, they thought it advisable to join the "state" church.

As the dominant provider of education – at first primary, and later, secondary – the colonial church was in an excellent position to transmit to succeeding generations of Caribbean peoples in the British Caribbean its own notions of morality, industry, and change. Because of its own commitment to political stability and its clientelic relationship with the colonial administration, the church found itself working in tandem with that administration to preserve the status quo. Politically, the church was conservative, if not reactionary; theologically, it was pietistic.

U.S. Missions

In more recent times U.S. missionaries have accompanied U.S. penetration of the Caribbean much as earlier missionaries accompanied earlier imperial powers. So, for example, no sooner had Puerto Rico become a U.S. colony (in 1898) than U.S. Protestant missionaries began to converge on the island. In fact, during the second half of 1899, secretaries of the Presbyterian, American Baptist, Congregational, and Methodist mission boards met to divide Puerto Rico into spheres of denominational missionary enterprise and influence.

In 1899, the American Baptists established a base at Rio Piedras, and Presbyterian missionaries established themselves at Mayaguez and San Juan. The United Brethren visited Ponce. The Methodists arrived in 1900, the Disciples of Christ in 1901, and the Congregationalists a year or two later. In 1902, missionaries of the Episcopal Church in the United States arrived and greatly helped the nascent Anglican Church that had been organized since 1873.

The Protestant churches, wittingly or otherwise, helped to make Puerto Rico "American" in outlook. Their religious and educational programs were conducted largely in English. Their congregations were modeled on those found in urban North America. The Protestant churches were middle-class in outlook, the morality they purveyed seemed to have been imported from the States without any alteration, and they were financed primarily from U.S. funding. All these factors gave the churches the appearance of propagating religious colonialism. Establishment of the Evangelical Seminary of Puerto Rico in 1919 provided for the training of local pastors, but modeled on a North American theological program, it could scarcely prepare them for an effective ministry in Puerto Rico. Similar missionary efforts occurred throughout the Caribbean.

Religious Cornucopia

The Caribbean region is a laboratory of religions and cults. The indigenous people of Guyana, the Amerindians, though largely Christianized, hold to beliefs that derive more from animism than from Christianity. African ideas and beliefs survive not only in such cultic expressions as vodun, or voodoo (Haiti), santería (Cuba), and shango (Trinidad and Tobago), but also in Revivalism and Bedwardism (Jamaica), the Jordanite movement (Guyana), and in the beliefs and practices of the Bush Negroes of Suriname.

The emancipation of slaves led to the importation of indentured Portuguese, Chinese, and Indian laborers into the Caribbean. Many Chinese became Christians, belonging mainly to the Roman Catholic and Anglican churches, except in Suriname, where they were generally Moravian. The Portuguese were Catholics before they came to the Caribbean. The immigrants from India were mainly Hindu although a significant number were Muslims. Large numbers of Hindus are to be found in Suriname, Guyana, and Trinidad; smaller numbers are to be found in Jamaica, Grenada, Guadeloupe, and Martinique. Significant numbers of Muslims (mainly of Indian extraction), can be found in Suriname, Trinidad, and Guyana.

In Martinique, the Maldevian cult represents a syncretism of Hindu beliefs and Christian teachings. African racial "national" aspirations combine with fundamentalist Protestant millenarianism to produce Rastafarianism among poorer, urbanized Jamaican blacks.

After the Jews were expelled from Spain in 1492, some settled in the Netherlands. From there they crossed the Atlantic and settled in Portuguese Brazil in the area around Pernambuco, which was captured by the Dutch in the 1630s. When the Dutch were expelled from Brazil in 1648, many Jews migrated to various parts of the Caribbean. Some went to the Dutch settlements of St. Eustatius and Curaçao around 1650; others went to Barbados. Today there are large congregations of Jews in Curaçao and Jamaica.

White Pentecostal preachers have popularized Pentecostal themes and have used the electronic media in modern times to propagate Pentecostalism in the Caribbean. Local converts, with frequent visits from noted U.S. evangelists, conducted tent crusades emphasizing speaking in tongues, the sins of the established churches, and the need for people to be "saved." As converts were recruited, Churches of God, Assemblies of God, and Full Gospel Fellowships sprang up in Caribbean countries as rivals to the established churches.

An interesting movement indigenous to Guyana is that of the White-Robed Army, or the Church of the West Evangelical Millennium Pilgrims (WEMP). The movement, whose followers are mainly blacks from the working class, combines beliefs and practices that derive from African traditional religions, Christianity, and Hinduism. It was the genius of Nathaniel Jordan (after whom members of the movement are sometimes called Jordanites) that wove an identifiable and coherent system of beliefs and practices from different strands of thought and practice.

Perhaps the best known of the religious expressions native to the Caribbean, however, are santería, vodun (voodoo), and Rastafarianism.

Santería (Saint Worship)

Although the Spanish Catholics were the first to teach Christianity to the blacks, their program could not be thorough, because there were never enough priests and missionaries to conduct an adequate mission among the slaves. The result was that in Cuba, many blacks learned enough of Catholic saints to identify them with their gods or to include them among their pantheon of divinities. That accommodation was facilitated by the belief that Catholic saints functioned as intermediaries between the Supreme God and humankind, in much the same way that the African divinities were believed to function as intermediaries between Oludumare, for example, and the Yorubas.

The cult that has grown up around the worship of the saints and African divinities in Cuba is called santería (saint worship). Santería cultists worship Ogun as Ogun Arere, the warrior; Ogun Oke, the hunter; and Ogun Aguanille, the metal worker. While Ogun may be the chief divinity of santería belief, the cultists combine the worship of this Yoruba divinity with that of other gods.

Vodun (Voodoo)

The Haitian vodunists retain the African belief in a supreme God whom they call *Le Bon Dieu. Le Bon Dieu* is believed to be well-disposed to humans and there is no need to worship him. Worship, however, is directed to the *loas* (spirits or divinities), which are sometimes referred to as *vodous, z'anges,* or *mysteres.*

The *loas* number in the hundreds. Many are identifiably African in origin, including Ogun, Damballa, Shango, Legba, Obatala, and Sousou Pannan. Others are identifiably Catholic saints, such as St. Anthony, St. Patrick, Papa Pie (St. Peter), and Mater Dolorosa (Mother of Sorrows, i.e., the Virgin Mary). For some Haitian peasants, the saints are identified with the divinities. Thus, Damballa is said to be St. Patrick, Legba is identified with St. Anthony, and Erzilie is said to be Mater Dolorosa.

On or about the vodun altar one will find crucifixes, rosaries, holy water, candles, and chromoliths of Catholic saints, mingled with thunder stones, flowers, flags, and food and liquors that are the gods' favorite. Elements of Catholic worship are integrated into the vodun worship service. Places where the spirits are believed to live are consecrated with holy water obtained from a Catholic church. The sprinkling of the water is invariably accompanied by the intonation of formulas that are Catholic in origin. A prayer at a vodun service may run:

> O Mary, Mother of Mercy, take pity on these poor abandoned souls. Mary, Mother of God, Mother of mothers, Mother of grace, pray for these converted souls, these souls of purgatory. All the saints, all the angels, angels of the heavens, gods of the water, gods of the forest, gods known and unknown, all the gods, all the twins, come and deliver this poor brother from tribulation. Do not permit bad spirits to spoil the service. And you, the dead, stop persecuting him. . . .

Most vodunists are also members of the Catholic Church. Their vodu priests (*houngans*) advise them to attend Mass regularly. But their understanding of the world around them is provided by vodun. In addition to the *loa* saints, their universe is peopled with the spirits of departed ancestors and by the "dead" generally – beliefs almost identical with their African forebears.

Rastafarianism

The Rastafarian movement is indigenous to Jamaica but has spread to other countries in the Anglophone Caribbean. It is sustained and pervaded by a sense of African triumphalism.

The Rastafarian doctrine that Haile Selassie is God was first preached in Kingston, Jamaica. When Ras Tafari was crowned as Haile Selassie, emperor of Ethiopia, in November 1930, Leonard P. Howell and other preachers recalled the words of Marcus Garvey that when a king was crowned in Africa, the time of the Africans' resurgence was near. Ethiopia came to be regarded as synonymous with Africa. Its symbolic value for blacks was powerful.

The religious motif was always present. It was God who would bring about the reversal of Africa's fortunes. A strong resemblance was perceived between the Africans and the Jews before the latter entered the Promised Land. The biblical passage "Ethiopia shall soon stretch forth her hand to God" became the text of many a sermon to be preached by blacks; it was regarded as a biblical prophecy that Africa would soon be redeemed. Meanwhile, the theme of Africa's resurgence was canvassed at Pan-African conferences and congresses. It was a subject close to the heart of Marcus Garvey, who, in the eyes of the blacks of western Kingston, Jamaica, had assumed the status of a prophet in the mold of Elijah or John the Baptist. When Ras Tafari was crowned Haile Selassie (which means "Power of the Trinity"), King of Kings, Lord of Lords, Conquering Lion of the Tribe of Judah, many poor blacks saw in the coronation the fulfillment of Garvey's prophecy that one day someone would arise in Africa who would unite the people of that continent into one nation.

The Rastafarians used their spiritual genius to translate the dreams of Garvey and the Pan-Africanists into the messianic and millenarian terms of the Bible. This gave the political utopianism of Garvey and others all the force and dynamism of a religious movement.

Rastafarianism preaches the overthrow of the present power structures (including the established churches) and the reversal of the present social order. Those presently disinherited and disadvantaged – the "sufferers" – will occupy positions of ease and power. Those who presently occupy such positions will become slaves and servants. Meanwhile, Rastafarians live according to the ethics of the anticipated millennium. They observe the food taboos of the ancient Hebrews; many of them are vegetarians. Many of them live by what they consider to be the Nazarite vow and refrain from shaving the face and consuming alcoholic beverages.

Rastas are to be found in Guyana, Trinidad and Tobago, Grenada, St. Vincent, Antigua, and Barbados. Whether the movement in these countries will achieve the significance it has in Jamaica remains to be seen.

Selected Bibliography for "Roots"

Augier, F. R., et al. *The Making of the West Indies.* Longman Caribbean, Ltd., 1960.

Barry, Thomas, et al. *The Other Side of Paradise: Foreign Control in the Caribbean.* New York: Grove Press, 1985.

Bisnauth, D. A. *A History of Religions in the Caribbean.* Kingston, Jamaica: Kingston Publishers, 1989.

———. *A Short History of the Guyana Presbyterian Church.* Georgetown, Guyana: Labour Advocate Printery, 1979.

Blackman, W. *Methodism: 200 Years in Barbados.* Bridgetown, Barbados, 1988.

Consultation for Ministry in a New Decade. Bridgetown, Barbados: Caribbean Conference of Churches, 1985.

Cuthbert, R. *Ecumenism and Development.* Bridgetown, Barbados, 1986.

Fagg, John E. *Cuba, Haiti and the Dominican Republic.* Englewood Cliffs, N.J.: Prentice-Hall, 1965.

Hamid, Idris, ed. *Troubling of the Waters.* San Fernando, Trinidad, 1973.

Jones, E., *Coalitions of the Oppressed.* Jamaica: ISER, University of the West Indies, 1987.

Langley, Lester D. *The United States and the Caribbean in the Twentieth Century.* 4th ed. Athens: University of Georgia Press, 1985.

Pantin, D. *Into the Valley of Debt.* Trinidad and Tobago, 1989.

Rohlehr, G. *Calypso and Society in Pre-Independence Trinidad.* Port-of-Spain, Trinidad, 1990.

Wheaton, P., and D. Shank. *Empire and the Word.* Washington, D.C.: EPICA, 1988.

ISSUES

6

Reclaiming Identity
The Verdun Proclamation

Preamble

The Caribbean/African American Dialogue (CAAD) and the Caribbean Conference of Churches (CCC) brought together representatives from throughout the Caribbean (including Suriname and Cayenne) and from North America and the United Kingdom in a consultation held at the Marian Retreat Center, in Verdun, Barbados, May 1–3, 1992. This consultation was the first Caribbean activity in the implementation of decisions taken at the First Inter-Continental Consultation of Indigenous, African/American, and African/Caribbean peoples on Racism in the Americas convened by the World Council of Churches in Rio de Janeiro in September 1990.

The Rio de Janeiro consultation had reflected on the meaning and challenge of 1992, the year of the fifth centennial of the arrival of Columbus in the Americas and the Caribbean, in the context of the search for a common vision for the future strategies of liberation of peoples "lest we endure another five hundred years of racism and dispossession."

The Caribbean/African American Dialogue does not separate itself from the challenge that confronts all dispossessed peoples of the hemisphere — indigenous, black, East Indian, "poor whites," nor indeed from responsibility to join the struggles of all the oppressed peoples of the world dramatically highlighted by the deeper significance of the 1992 anniversary, as we seek to reverse the course of our marginalization which both symbolically and realistically may be considered to have begun in 1492.

The consultation paused to reflect on these five hundred years and agreed that looking back should not be an exercise in self-pity, nor in the pathological discarding of our responsibility for our own salvation at the present time when political independence has been achieved in the majority of the Caribbean countries and political power is in the hands of the people. We look back in order to sharpen our consciousness of our historical condition, thereby to better understand our present existential realities and to better chart the course for our total liberation and self-realization.

The consultation looked at the dominant factors in the historical condition of the Caribbean. For example, racism and imperialistic economic domination had entered into a symbiotic relationship in the founding of New World societies and had assumed grotesque proportions. They continue to underlie the contemporary realities of the Caribbean and the Third World in general although they have acquired a new complex set of dimensions, with class for example coming to intersect with race as the focus of economic exploitation.

The consultation also recognized positives in the resourcefulness and resilience of Caribbean peoples as they created cultural systems of religion, worldview, and language not only to order their daily lives, but also as instruments of resistance, rebellion, and survival. The Haitian revolution was particularly seen as an important act, but one among many others of self-liberation which have abounded in the post-Columbian Caribbean historical experience. These acts of self-liberation gave freedom to a greater number of persons than those who were freed by colonial edict. The consultation observed that the Caribbean would do well to consider whether at the present time, rather than the quincentennial of Columbus's adventure, it is the bicentennial of the Haitian revolution that should be the significant anniversary.

As we face the prospect of the emergence of a monolithic capitalist global village, it becomes even more urgent for the dialogue to continue among Caribbean peoples (and indeed among Third World peoples in general) to determine our own place, on our negotiated terms, in the new dispensation. We want to continue to deepen our knowledge and understanding of our condition, refocusing the role which racism and capitalism have historically played in genocide, economic deprivation and marginalization, family disruptions, and personal and cultural alienation, and to prepare ourselves to withstand the continuing dehumanization which we may expect from the unbridled, neo-liberal free market systems which Caribbean governments seem poised to adopt.

This leads to the question: How do we escape the throes of helplessness, hopelessness, alienation, and dehumanization now besetting the Caribbean? Without pretending to have definitive answers, the consultation examined a number of issues and defined a modest set of actions and measures to which participants committed themselves.

Racism

Xenophobia and racism seem to be inherent to human nature. Throughout the history of humanity men have as individuals or as groups always resented, feared, or resisted the presence of or the intrusion of other men or groups, just because they were foreigners or different.

It was in the sixteenth century, when the development of the mercantile system gave birth to capitalism, that racism really took a new dimension as a concept whereby one ethnic group (namely the black Africans) were labelled genetically inferior on the basis of their different origins and color of skin.

Within the decade that followed the intrusion of Columbus into this part of the world, most of the indigenous populations had been exterminated by the European conquistadors in their ravenous lust for gold.

It then became a "vital necessity" from their viewpoint to capitalize on an availability of cheap labor to improve and increase their production. In order to mitigate the plight of the "Indians," the church endorsed the trade in Africans as slaves.

Measures were deliberately and methodically taken by legislative authority of the political powers to perpetuate this exploitation and oppression.

Black Africans were classified as subhuman, just above the animal – "a tabula rasa" devoid of intellect and soul; thus they could be sold as cattle. The Christian churches played their part in this dehumanizing process. The color of the African skin was interpreted by religious authorities as living proof that Africans were cursed by God. To put a seal on the matter, neither intellectual capacity nor the spiritual life of the Africans was recognized. As a consequence both the so-called superior race and the so-called inferior one came to internalize these beliefs about themselves, designed by the white European.

When the European powers invaded Asia and Africa in the nineteenth century, although the driving force behind them was their desire to acquire wealth and assert supremacy, they professed that the white man's burden was to civilize.

Today, five centuries after the intrusion, new peoples have come, slavery has been "abolished" at least physically, and most of the region is enjoying political independence.

Still racism is never far away. Its hideous face shows itself more and more openly, the *alter ego* of human greed and lust for power over the many for the few who have capital. The dehumanizing process takes so many forms: We keep repeating the same self-debasing sayings and proverbs about ourselves and our skin color; we keep on having the same self-destructive attitudes toward ourselves and our people, persistently seeking the Europeans' seal before we accept recognition of ourselves as an able, talented people, and endorsing and perpetuating the same evils against our resident minorities; our women are overworked and underpaid in the world of commerce; our Haitian brothers endure seemingly endless suffering; worst of all we make ourselves guilty of initiating among or against our oppressed fellow human beings the same patterns of racial hostility from which we ourselves have so direly suffered.

Even if European civilization in dealing with other civilizations does not, as it should, get rid of the prejudices that have dehumanized Europeans as much as their ex-slaves, surely it is high time we ourselves break away from a Eurocentric framework and move into a humane design of civilization as subjects of our own destiny, with pride in our past and in the achievements of our resistance, with pride in our survival and in the great contributions we have made to humanity.

Indeed it is time we put into practice the call of this Kreyol poem:

Yo tire tannou	They took what was ours
Yo bannou ta yo	They gave us theirs
Nou Ka tire ta yo	We are removing theirs
No ka pwan tannou	We are taking ours back
Nou ka Libere nou	We are liberating ourselves.

Caribbean Cultural Identity

A people's culture is their way of life as formed by their own historical experience in their own geographical environment. It therefore becomes immediately clear that a Caribbean cultural identity is an indisputable reality. Born of displacement, resistance, and survival, it is a cultural identity attested to in our creolization of both the languages and lifestyles adopted from Europe and our (often too) ready adaptability to their models; attested to also in the significantly open-air aspects of our lifestyle, in the percussive character and notable folk-rhythm of our music, in the catching sensuality of our dancing, in our pervasive religiosity, and so on.

Most of these characteristics are markedly underpinned by a black African ethos which spreads across all the Euro-determined national and linguistic boundaries of the Caribbean and has established a certain unity, definable as Caribbean, in the diversity of territorial or insular subcultures of the region. To that basic unifying design have been added significant Asiatic elements, mostly East Indian and to a lesser degree Chinese, together with, mostly on the rimland continental territories, remainder elements of our aboriginal predecessors – Arawak, Carib, and Maya – the only truly indigenous Caribbean peoples.

Caribbean culture has therefore developed out of the dynamic cross-fertilization of all the world's major races – Amerindian, Caucasian, African, Indic, Chinese – each today a recognizable limb of an egalitarian stock which is unmatched anywhere else on earth. It has provided a conglomerate heritage that in some ways leads the world, as in the historically unsurpassed Amerindian respect for the environment, or in present-day musical inventiveness as shown by the Trinidadian steel band, or in flashes of sporting supremacy as on the cricket field. In other ways, benefiting from the natural gift of perennial sunshine, it has created its own kind of colorful festivals – Carnival, Kadooment, Jonkonnu, Mashramani, etc. – that have each a peculiar power to galvanize cooperative communities of friendship out of rank strangers, so much so that this Caribbean cultural skill has become a welcome import in the friendless mega-cities of Britain and North America.

There is a heritage, too, of vital skills and of values developed through a long Caribbean history of enforced adversity, skills of harnessing the environment for survival, whether of flavoring and preserving foods or of gaining medicines from bush; values of respect anxiously sought but morally earned among one's peers and then keenly cherished; and values of responsibility to the extended family.

Caribbean culture has therefore emerged creatively as an identifiable entity, even if a loose one, out of a harshly repressive past. The CARIFESTA experiences since 1972 have shown the immense potential that culture has for bringing and binding together Caribbean peoples of every race and nationality. If for that reason alone, we must proudly preserve it. If for that reason alone, we must strongly defend it from being penetrated and damaged by mass media and other forces from external cultures, some simply uncaring but some purposefully programmed to distract and destroy or to dissolve and absorb, but by whichever means ultimately to control us without choice or chance of resistance.

In order to strengthen ourselves for such defense we need to address and discard some of the aspects of our historical heritage which are negative – a ready self-effacement before a Euro-American product or model, a propensity for skin-shade preferences or rationalized racism, mistaken notions of self-preservation in the form of parochialism or insularity, and perhaps worst of all the fostering of paramountcy and rajaship by or around those we entrust with the authority of leadership.

We must agree and resolve then to attack and remove those rooted diseases from our present condition, while so nurturing that conglomerate Caribbean stock that is our basic culture as to make it flourish even if civilization does become a global village, vitally lighting up our own corner of it, and contributing as much rich color to it as it chooses itself to receive from the whole.

Economic Democracy

The question of economic democracy is a question of justice. It has to do with people being able to reproduce the conditions of their existence in ways that bring security and rising standards of living; it means progress and dignity. The historical condition of existence of Caribbean and African-American people has been one rooted in the contradiction between the economic and political spheres of social existence: on the one hand, the arbitrary separation of economics from politics and, on the other, the acceptance of economic inequality in co-existence with claims of formal political equality. This artificial separation has given rise to economic injustice and political oppression and regression.

Injustice associated with hunger, want, deprivation and economic insecurity result not from economic shortages per se, but from a lack of justice. The absence of freedom and justice results from social systems that elevate greed and possessive individualism to the status of values while devaluing the needs of the collective community. This has been the result of making the state into the servant, not of individual interests, but of powerful and privileged factions that come to dominate society.

Economic democracy rests on the idea of the reordering of the priorities of the state and society. It calls for decentralizing decision-making and allowing for the creation and development of institutions in society through which groups at the community level are free to develop their potential, not merely for survival but for full living. It means the conditions under which economic insecurity, injustice, deprivation, scarcity, and terminal poverty are overcome and where justice, freedom, and human dignity become the norm. It means treating the resources of society as patrimony, as a trust of the people in perpetuity. It means gender equality, not merely in law, but also in the structures through which the roles of women in economic production, biological reproduction, sexuality, and socialization are transformed through the abolition of patriarchal domination of society's resources and of women's lives. It means sensitivity to the environment and an end to environmental degradation, a new compact between humans and nature. Economic democracy is impossible under discrimination based on racial, ethnic, or national origin; it is incompatible with religious intolerance or any form of national chauvinism.

Therefore, for Caribbean peoples who have suffered these many centuries and whose descendants still bear the mark of oppression and exploitation, economic democracy demands nothing less than land reform so that appropriate strategies may be implemented with a design to feed the people. It demands popular participation in decision-making with a view toward industrial development strategies that result in meaningful employment. The objective is to develop skills and harness the productive energies of the people. Economic democracy for Caribbean peoples requires educational programs geared to the needs of the modern world economy. This calls for curriculum redevelopment. Economic democracy in the Caribbean must take into account the tenuousness in the relationship between sovereignty as a legal factor and autonomy as the capacity not only to design but to effectively implement strategies deemed appropriate for the survival of the nation. Given the small economic scale of Caribbean economy and society, the pursuit of economic democracy demands nothing less than the effective integration of the fragmented Caribbean nation and the building of appropriate linkages across the diaspora, for we are a nation without borders.

Towards a Caribbean Theology

The encounter of two worlds which began with Columbus's entry into the Caribbean was the beginning of a struggle for survival which continues to this day. The European colonization of the Caribbean and the Americas has led to the near annihilation of the original peoples who inhabited these islands, the enslavement of millions of Africans to replace the indigenous population, and the arrival of thousands of Asians from India and to a lesser extent China. All these persons were important for one thing, and that was to provide the labor force necessary for creating wealth for the colonizers.

The one factor which allowed the peoples of the Caribbean to survive was their belief systems or religion. These religious beliefs and practices gave these people, especially the African population, the fortitude they needed to withstand the dehumanizing practices of the Europeans. This, however, does not mean that our people have come out unscathed. The peoples of the Caribbean continue to suffer the trauma of that wretched system.

The religious mosaic of the Caribbean presents the world with the most interesting feature to be found any place in the world. Here we have a very curious blending of African and European religious practices. What is so interesting in this meeting of religions is the fact that although the Europeans used all sorts of forces, physical and psychological, to wipe out the beliefs and practices of Africans, they have not succeeded, and these beliefs and practices continue to live on (even if not in their pure forms) and have altered Christianity, the religion of the Europeans.

In spite of the unique character of the Caribbean, the worldview which dominates the region is still very much Eurocentric. The existence of many religious beliefs and practices does not mean the acceptance of all of them. Those which are accepted are the ones the Europeans have approved. Afrocentric religious beliefs are still considered evil, and even where there is religious tolerance there is still a great deal of suspicion. Except for students of anthropology, sociology, and history, little effort has been made to understand the religious beliefs and practices with an African base. The officials of the Christian churches do not recognize a need for dialogue with these religious beliefs, even when there is conflict between what the churches teach and what the people believe.

The fact that the Christian churches, which by and large are led by clergy who are the descendants of Africans, do not see any value in carrying on dialogue with the religious beliefs and practices found among African peoples goes to show the extent to which prejudice against Africans has been instilled within the peoples of the Caribbean. It also confirms how very Eurocentric the churches are in their thinking.

Today one witnesses an even more aggressive attack on the religious practices of African Caribbean peoples and to some extent the religious practices of the peoples of Indian origin. These religious practices are termed cults and are said to be of satanic origin. This new wave of attack comes from biblical fundamentalists originating in the Bible belt of the U.S.A., some of which have political agendas.

With the advent of modern means of communication, especially the electronic media, we witness a set of values which can be considered foreign to the region. Caribbean peoples are now being exposed to lifestyles that are unsuitable and unaffordable. These newly found ways of living are destroying the very fabric of the society and are causing governments to turn to international lending agencies to pay wages and balance budgets. These agencies then impose measures on the countries which deprive poor people of what is necessary for comfortable living.

What the people of the Caribbean need, if they are to progress in a meaningful way, is a shift in focus. The Eurocentric worldview has done untold harm to the Caribbean psyche and continues to undermine the people's self-confidence where they are constantly seeking the approval of others. Caribbean people do not have the confidence in themselves which would enable them to seek solutions to Caribbean problems in the Caribbean itself. That self-confidence will come about when they are able to reject a Eurocentric worldview.

The role of the churches in assisting in the bringing about of a Eurocentric worldview has not been a minor one. The churches have contributed and continue to contribute to such a view. If the churches are to break with Eurocentrism, then they must be prepared to question their theology, which is the foundation for Eurocentrism.

When we look at the theological thinking behind slavery and even emancipation, it was not to liberate the Africans but to "civilize" them, which really meant getting them to be totally submissive to the colonizers. The movements for liberation were not led by the religious thinkers and in many instances came under heavy criticism from the churches. Today the churches cannot claim to be at the forefront in the quest for total liberation. Most of those at the center are persons who either do not adhere to the churches' teachings or are marginalized by church authorities.

During this year of the Quincentenary when some are preparing to celebrate Columbus's entry into the Caribbean, one can see subtle forms of confirming the Eurocentric worldview. Even the churches, by observing five hundred years of evangelization while ignoring what those five hundred years have been for indigenous American and African peoples, are knowingly or unknowingly contributing to such a view.

If the churches in the Caribbean feel that they should in some way mark the Quincentenary, they should use a totally different approach. The churches should be calling on the theologians in the region to start a process of theological reflection which would enable the peoples of the region to reject totally the suggestion that the world is Eurocentric. Today, when there is a call for a New World Order, it is imperative that Caribbean theologians come to realize that any idea of a New World Order is incomplete if it excludes the views of non-European peoples and particularly if Caribbean thinking is excluded.

Caribbean Integration

Already divided by reason of insularity, language, immigration legislation, and the isolationist policies of powerful nations, the Caribbean countries are now faced with a tendency on the part of

European, Pacific, and North American nations to form themselves into multilateral blocs – e.g., the European Community, the Japan bloc, and the North American Free Trade Agreement (NAFTA) – for the purpose of the global integration of capital.

In order to balance their own economic situations the Caribbean nations have attached themselves to multilateral blocs through such organizations as the Caribbean Basin Initiative (CBI) and Enterprise for the Americas (U.S. administrations); CARIBCAN (a Caribbean-Canadian development agency for the East Caribbean); GATT (the General Agreement on Tariffs and Trade); and the Lomé Convention (on economic policies with the Third World).

As a result, the Caribbean region finds itself economically and politically weakened from without through more and more dependence for its support and existence upon the manipulations of these multilateral blocs and intra-regionally by the lack of Caribbean unity, weakness in communication, and a generally insular manner of existence.

These factors, among others, point to the need for the nations of the Caribbean to seek to become united and integrated as the only means of insuring their viable existence in the future.

As Caribbean people we share a common heritage with our dispossessed counterparts scattered throughout the continents and countries outside the Caribbean.

Therefore, as Caribbean people, we affirm our heritage and determine to communicate through (a) people-to-people exchanges, (b) cultural art forms, (c) documentation, (d) exchange of information, (e) regular meetings and consultations, (f) joint planning and implementation of programs, (g) sports, and (h) integration as one Caribbean nation, to celebrate and affirm our survival and pool resources to effectively address issues affecting our ability to LIVE!

Resolutions

1. We resolve that this consultation endorse the statement coming out of the First Inter-Continental Consultation of Indigenous, African/American, and African/Caribbean peoples on Racism in the Americas held in Rio de Janeiro, Brazil, in September 1990.

We further resolve that the participants of this consultation will take the message of Rio to the entire Caribbean community.

2. We resolve to carry the findings of this consultation to our various communities and to the hemispheric consultation to be held in the Bahamas in August 1992.

3. We resolve to work to strengthen the unity of the Caribbean and to join forces with other agencies, governmental and nongovernmental, with similar goals.

4. We resolve to join with African Americans in the U.S.A., South America, Canada, and Central America, as well as with people of African origin living in Britain and other European countries, for the cultural, spiritual, and economic advancement of our people who have been displaced and dispossessed by slavery, racism, and colonialism and who continue to suffer all forms of dehumanization.

   We further resolve to cooperate with the indigenous people of the Caribbean and the Americas and other dispossessed peoples as well as persons and organizations working for the liberation of the poor people of the world.

5. We resolve to endorse the decision of the World Council of Churches to covenant a day of prayer and ask the World Council of Churches to designate October 12th, 1992, as that day of prayer. We further resolve that October 12th, 1992, be declared a Universal Day of Hope.

Calls

1. We call upon the churches in the Caribbean to work for the eradication of all forms of racism and to campaign vigorously for the liberation of indigenous people in Caribbean states.

2. We call upon the churches of the Caribbean to work for the creation of a Caribbean theology, one which will liberate Caribbean people from a Eurocentric worldview.

3. We call upon the governments and peoples of the Caribbean to express solidarity with the peoples of Cuba as an economic war is being waged against that country.

4. We call upon the people, churches, and governments of the Caribbean to pursue actions to secure the implementation of the OAS accord and the return of the legitimate government of Haiti.

5. We call upon the Caribbean community to recognize the right of Puerto Rico to self-determination.

6. We call upon the Caribbean community to work for a multi-lingual community which would make it easier for Caribbean people to communicate with each other.

7. We call upon the governments of nations of the Caribbean to make it easier to travel around the region (cheaper air fares, removal of visa requirements).

As Caribbean peoples we reject the attempt to glorify 1492 without asking pardon of indigenous Caribbean and American peoples and peoples of African and Asian origin who have been brutally treated as a result of the encounter and who to this day continue to suffer the effects of it.

As a Caribbean people who have survived the Middle Passage we affirm all the positive things that have survived, such as our rich cultural heritage, our religious traditions, our deep sense of the family, and our respect for other peoples. We will work to bring about changes in the economic order which would lead to the proper development of our people, and we also will work to recover these elements of our culture that are being eroded by the deliberate design of external forces through the use of the powerful electronic media and politically motivated religious groups.

We are committed to the building of a new Caribbean, a Caribbean which does not exclude any nation or state nor any language group. We embrace all the members of our Caribbean family.

We are totally committed to working with African Americans in North America, Central America, and South America as well as with Africans in Mother Africa and the Diaspora for the eradication of racism, and to building bridges of friendship with indigenous Caribbean and American peoples, peoples from the subcontinent of Asia, and indeed all oppressed people of the World.

We are committed to the building of a New World, a world built on justice and peace, and we demand that we be given every opportunity to assist in the creation of this New World.

7

The Seamy Side of Paradise

by Dale A. Bisnauth

In Jamaica, at Dunn's River beach in St. Ann on the north coast, or in Montego Bay and Bluefields, one can appreciate why so many tourists come to visit. With beautiful sandy beaches, the emerald sea, and the warm tropical sun, the island is a tourist paradise — breathtakingly beautiful. Add to sun, sea, and sand the "friendly natives," and you have a tourist's dream.

In Guyana, the beauty of the tropical vegetation is matched by the architecture of the old, wooden colonial-type buildings in Georgetown and New Amsterdam. The Kaieteur Falls, the Pakaraima mountains, the Essequibo River all have their appeal.

Trinidad offers the northern mountains or panoramic views of Port-of-Spain from one's hotel.

The brochures provided by travel agencies do not exaggerate the beauty of Caribbean countries. On one island, swift cool streams run down to the sea, providing an unusual treat of freshwater bathing; on another, miles of beautiful unspoiled beaches and concealed bays offer a wealth of privacy and peace.

Antigua has hundreds of secluded bays and inlets, fringed by coral reefs and white sand beaches. Barbados has shops and department stores lining Broad and Swan Streets in Bridgetown, and excellent specialty shops and boutiques have sprung up along the Christchurch and St. James coasts.

No, the literature does not exaggerate the beauty of the "pearls" of the Caribbean archipelago; it simply fails to mention that there is another side to the Caribbean paradise — a side that the tourists who confine themselves to beach, sea, hotel, shopping mall, and fast-foods outlet may never even be aware of. And the "friendly natives," from the finely muscled "beach-boys" to the uniformed hotel

employees, are not likely to tell about that other side of paradise —
where they live. After all, tourism means money and employment.
Who would want to sell their country short by exposing the seamy
side of paradise?

The stark truth is that the Caribbean is a region of pervasive and
persistent poverty. It is undoubtedly culturally rich. There are sec-
tions of the population that are comfortably well off; some people
are very wealthy. But the masses of Caribbean peoples struggle just
at or below the bread line. A crisis in a national economy can mean
disaster for many people.

A number of factors have contributed to this poverty. The Caribbean nations emerged in the 1960s with a sense of buoyancy and
hope after years of colonialism and dictatorship. Announcing that
"Massa Day Done," Caribbean political leaders took their people
into the era of independence with such confidence that it seemed
the transition from pre-industrial, economically dependent, primary
producers to modern, developed countries with viable economies
would follow as a matter of course. The traditional agriculture-based
economies began to open up to include mining (Jamaica, Guyana,
Suriname), petroleum (Trinidad and Tobago), banking, tourism, and
manufacturing.

But after the Indian summer of high prices for Caribbean sugar
and bananas in the 1960s, the Caribbean nations faced sinking
prices for exports, shrinking markets, rising interest rates on debts,
and increasing costs for oil and other imports. These, in turn, meant
a halt to plans for industrialization and a growing impoverishment
reflected in growing unemployment and social malaise. Caribbean
peoples learned that political independence did not carry with it
economic autonomy and viability.

Caribbean economies are small, dependent, and really at the
mercy of what happens to the economies of those industrialized
countries to which they are tied. Thus, many a Caribbean country
experienced an economic boom in the 1960s. In the 1970s and
1980s, however, Caribbean economies suffered badly with the recession in the industrialized countries, caused by meteoric increases
in oil prices in the 1970s. The volume of trade between the Caribbean and the industrialized North dropped; but at the same time,
the deficit in the Caribbean trade with the industrialized countries
increased as the Caribbean exported less but imported goods at
higher costs.

The Burden of Debt

There was a dramatic increase in the debt burden of most Caribbean countries in the 1970s, except for Trinidad and Tobago, which had oil. Caribbean countries had incurred debts as part of their process of development. But they have had to pursue that development in a hostile external economic and commercial environment and have experienced economic stagnation at the same time that they have increased their indebtedness.

At the heart of the debt crisis has been the fact that Caribbean countries experienced a decline in their export earnings due to the recession in the industrialized countries. That recession led to a decline in demand and falling prices for the Caribbean staples – sugar, bananas, coffee, citrus, bauxite, and aluminum. The recession also triggered the rise of strong protectionist practices on the part of industrialized countries that have frustrated Caribbean efforts to promote exports of non-traditional products. Add to this the fact that Caribbean countries have had to face inflation in the price of imports from industrialized countries, and it can be appreciated that they are truly caught in a debt trap of increasing negative balances in trade as well as in current accounts. They are forced into increasing debt to finance these negative balances. Then they are forced to incur additional debts to retire pre-existing debts and to build up capital and finance investments.

Debts have to be serviced. Debt-servicing has imposed a heavy strain on the Caribbean countries. Some have to earmark between 10 and 25 percent of their export earnings for debt servicing; for other countries, debt servicing can take as much as 40 to 50 percent. This means less money for national development.

At the end of 1985, Cuba, the Dominican Republic, and Jamaica had outstanding external debts exceeding US$3 billion each, with Jamaica's (US$3.587 billion) being the largest. These debts have increased substantially since then. Debt as a percentage of the national Gross Domestic Product presents the picture in more dramatic terms. In 1985, Guyana's debt was 239.1 percent of its GDP; Jamaica's, 177.6 percent of that country's GDP; the Dominican Republic's, 71.6 percent; and Grenada's, 51.6 percent. Debt service as a percentage of earnings from the export of goods and services in Jamaica was 36.5 percent; in Cuba, 32.4 percent; in Grenada, 20.3 percent; and in Haiti, 18.7 percent.

Meanwhile, nearly all Caribbean countries have had negative balances on merchandise trade. For all their borrowing, Caribbean countries have not shown any significant development. The region's economists have declared that if the countries were to be stripped of their many imported goods – automobiles, video sets, televisions, and so on – the countries would resemble what they were a century ago: plantation societies with sugar cane, bananas, and cocoa. Nowadays, there are a few mines scattered throughout the region and some countries have gone into tourism in a big way. Such changes that have taken place have been little more than a transition from the "pure plantation economy" (1600–1838), to the "modified plantation economy (1839–1938), and finally, to the "further modified plantation economy" (1939 to the present). The persistence of the plantation economy in which a few rich families control how the loans are spent has led to continuing underdevelopment and poverty.

In the Dominican Republic, for all its tobacco, rum distilling, coffee, and sugar processing industries, and its famous Carnivals, most of the peasants who live in rural areas exist in oppressive poverty where unemployment is over 50 percent, illiteracy 80 percent, and malnutrition epidemic. Forty percent of that country's wealth is controlled by 6 percent of the population, and a handful of foreign-based transnational corporations control every sector of the economy.

Haiti remains one of the most destitute places in the world, and Guyana is said to be even poorer than Haiti. Two or three of the poorest nations in the hemisphere are Caribbean countries.

Which Way Out?

Once it seemed that there were three alternatives for the Caribbean nations:

1. Countries could opt for nationalist programs that would promote more local ownership of resources and industries;

2. Countries could follow Cuba and break with the international capitalist system; or

3. Countries could open up their economies even further to foreign trade and investment with the hope that the benefits from

foreign-owned operations would trickle down into the local economy.

Jamaica and Guyana followed the first alternative but came to grief because of foreign pressure and internal problems. Caribbean countries now fight shy of nationalization or of wanting to control the commanding heights of the economy. Nobody wants to risk the internal upheaval and international pressure that the socialist approach of the second alternative would entail, particularly since socialism, with the breakup of the Soviet Union and its economy, has been seriously discredited. The path of dependent capitalism seems to be the only viable alternative for development open to Caribbean countries.

Many (if not most) Caribbean political directorates have now completely opened up their countries to foreign investment and trade. These countries now boast of ERPs – Economic Recovery Programs – even as they increase their traditional reliance on the developed countries. The region has become one of the world's areas most penetrated by transnational corporations. This can be attributed to three factors:

1. Pressure from the Reagan and Bush administrations;

2. Inability of the region's governments to formulate an economic strategy of their own; and

3. Pressure of conditions stipulated by the International Monetary Fund (IMF) before it makes foreign exchange loans available to debtor countries (so they can meet their debt obligations and fulfill the demands of foreign investors and suppliers of foreign exchange).

The United States offered a panacea to the Caribbean economic ills in the form of the Caribbean Basin Initiative, first announced in 1982. According to President Reagan, the CBI would provide emergency funds and would open the U.S. market to products from the Caribbean and Central America. The opening up of the U.S. market was perceived as the main solution of the region's woes.

To date, the Caribbean Basin Initiative has had little impact on the region's economy. Funds made available by the CBI have been low and they have been tied to America's strategic interest; the U.S. market has permitted entry on a duty-free basis to only 7 percent of the region's exports. The type of industrialization stimulated by the CBI (mainly export substitutions) has not contributed in a significant way to capital formation and accumulation in the region, nor has it eased, let alone solved, the problems of unemployment and poverty. However, it has laid the foundations to restore the Caribbean Basin's attractiveness to U.S. capital. The principal beneficiaries of this kind of investment would be U.S. corporations that have plants in the Caribbean and have access to cheap Caribbean labor.

Tourism

A bright spot in the Caribbean economy in recent times – tourism – has been a mixed blessing. For most Caribbean countries, tourism has been the single most important economic activity and the major earner of hard currency. Since 1984, tourist arrivals from North America and Europe have increased. The industry has been the leading foreign exchange earner in Jamaica, Barbados, Antigua, St. Lucia, the Bahamas, and other Caribbean countries, although not all the tourist dollars spent on the islands remain there to fuel local economic development. It is estimated that for every dollar spent in the Bahamas, 81 cents find its way back to the United States, and 90 percent of Antigua's tourism is controlled by the predominantly foreign private sector. However, many Caribbean governments rely on the tourist dollars to keep their economies afloat, to balance their budgets, and to buy their imports.

And tourism helps to alleviate unemployment, providing over a quarter million jobs in the Caribbean, ranging from 2 percent of the work force in Jamaica to about 70 percent in Bermuda. Women who are employed as maids, waitresses, kitchen help, desk clerks, and so on fill as many as 75 percent of jobs – not including less respectable activities related to the entertainment of male visitors.

But the benefits that Caribbean countries derive from tourism can hardly compare with those that accrue to the transnational corporations for which tourism is big business, second only to petroleum. In the Caribbean, transnational corporations (TNCs) such as TWA and ITT have controlled the development of tourism and have reaped the bulk of the industry's profits. Large foreign firms are involved in every phase of the industry: airlines, hotels, services, and tour operators. Tourists on prepaid tours spend almost all of their holiday allowance in their home country long before they set foot on a Caribbean island. Because of the transnational nature of tourism, payments for services rendered in the Caribbean pass directly to the New York headquarters of Sheraton or Hertz, without even passing through the agency offices in the Caribbean.

An increasing number of tourists are now coming to the Caribbean in cruise ships. These ships linger for just as long as it takes passengers to do some quick shopping on shore. The cruise-liner business contributes about 5 percent of the foreign-exchange earnings of the region's tourism industry. Whether this is adequate compensation for the environmental damage done to Caribbean waters by the effluent dumped by these ships is debatable.

If tourism is big business, it is also subsidized business. Multinational lending institutions and foreign and local governments build roads, expand airports, and offer tax incentives for investment in tourism. Infrastructural improvements are made with tourists in mind. In the end, it is the locals who have to pay for these improvements, not the tourism industry.

As tourists from North America and Europe descend on these small countries, they can outnumber the local residents. Thus the number of annual stop-over visitors to the United States Virgin Islands is seven times the local population! And visitors can put a heavy strain on an island's infrastructure. In Barbados, tourists use 1.6 times as much water and sewers as Barbadians and more than 27 times as much electricity.

But governments invest in the industry. Sometimes land that could be put to agriculture to feed the local population is used for golf courses, roads to hotels, hotel expansion, and other infrastructural purposes related to the tourism industry. At other times, shore-line ecological systems are destroyed, with serious consequences for marine and fish life, in order that marinas may be built for tourist pleasure. And where use is hardly made of local supplies, including food items, a country's import bill may escalate on account of the tourism industry. Thus, in Guadeloupe, imports account for about 80 percent of the total cost of hotel supplies.

Far from sharing in the local culture, cuisine, and ambiance of the Caribbean, the tourism industry has led to the strengthening of a Caribbean trait: to mimic the foreigners, from their consumerist ways to their love for disco music. Tourism undoubtedly has its benefits, but when it converts a people's habitat into a playground, it also converts that people's farmers into waiters and its fishermen into beach boys. And when the playboys and playgirls are mostly white and those that cater to their pleasure invariably black, it creates a situation that can turn ugly.

Society in Peril

The Caribbean is an archipelago under threat. Between June and November every year, there is the threat from hurricanes. A hurricane such as Gilbert, which struck Jamaica and Puerto Rico recently, can destroy a country's agriculture and damage its infrastructure severely. Serious as this threat is, there are others that are worse. These are related to the region's social and cultural integrity. In the Anglophone Caribbean, where the culture is most tenuous because of its history, some fear what they describe as the social and cultural "de-Caribbeanization" of the region.

The redefinition of the local culture by tourism is strengthened by other activities in the region, including illicit drug trade and substance abuse, U.S. satellite television programs and short-wave radio bombardment, popular U.S. tabloids that purvey an inappropriate consumerist lifestyle for Caribbean peoples and U.S.-based sectarian religious movements, some with political or social agendas.

Whether these activities represent a conscious attempt to bring the Caribbean under the cultural and social hegemony of the United States or whether they represent the inevitable social and cultural dimension of a political and economic hegemony that has already been established, the result is the same: Caribbean states face the real possibility of being little more than cultural extensions of the United States of America. The saddest aspect of this process is that Caribbean governments and significant sectors of Caribbean populations have been active collaborators in the region's cultural impoverishment.

Cultural dislocation is one result of the persistent poverty that pervades the region, but another is migration. Haitian migration to the Bahamas, the Dominican Republic, the U.S. Virgin Islands, and other Caribbean countries has created many problems and has raised questions related to human rights and the just treatment of migrant groups. Migrants and political refugees have gone in substantial numbers into Belize, Suriname, and other countries. Movements from country to town, usually in search of employment, have resulted in the heavy urbanization of populations in Puerto Rico, the Dominican Republic, Barbados, Jamaica, and other states, putting additional strain on social and infrastructural services. Meanwhile, external migration, mainly to the United States and Canada, has created a serious "brain drain" and critical shortages in medical sciences, engineering, and other technically oriented fields, as well as in management and skilled crafts.

Migration, in whatever direction, has added to the severe disruption of families already under stress, because both parents, and sometimes younger children, have to earn in order that a family may survive economic pressures. The stress has been greater on women, not only those who are heads of single-parent families (and these are growing in number), but also those who have become informal traders and entrepreneurs in economies where men held these roles.

While social dislocations have resulted in a rising incidence of crimes of violence against the person, dislocations within the family have given rise to domestic violence in which women and children are the victims. Meanwhile, the incapacity of local economies to absorb the graduates of schools and universities means that the numbers of the unemployed younger people are growing. Some of these are vulnerable to the temptations of the illicit trade in drugs.

Politically, some of the countries are volatile. In 1991, there was a violent coup attempt on the government of A. N. R. Robinson of Trinidad and Tobago. Recently, Jean-Bertrand Aristide, the first elected president of Haiti, was ousted by the army in a land where coups are a regular occurrence. Suriname has had its coups. Puerto Rico, the French Caribbean, and the Dominican Republic have had their share of violent incidents related to politics. Jamaica has known killings around times of election. St. Kitts experienced fire-bombings as a result of feuds between political parties. Guyana experienced brutal human rights violations, political repression, and killings under the Forbes Burnham regime. With key policemen and officers trained in Washington and equipped there as well, some Anglophone Caribbean governments have forces that they can use on internal and external enemies.

Large trading blocs are developing in other parts of the world, but the Caribbean's movement toward regionalism is not proceeding as fast as the urgency of its economic needs would seem to demand. Old rivalries are dying hard, while new rivalries for

common external markets and identical sources of external funding impede the progress toward political, economic, and cultural
integrity in a competitive world. All is far from being well in
paradise!

8

Foreign Debt and the Drug Trade

Declaration of Kingston

**Document of the Second Encounter of Bishops
and Pastors from Latin America and the Caribbean
Kingston, Jamaica, June 4–9, 1990**

*"Sowing seeds of hope
after a decade of despair"*

"When my people in their need look for water,
when their throats are dry with thirst,
then I, the Lord, will answer their prayer;
I, the God of Israel, will never abandon them."
(Isa. 41:17)

Introduction

Assembled in common faith in the Lord Jesus Christ, we bishops, pastors, and consultants from the Caribbean and Latin America, from the United States, Canada, and Europe, met in Kingston, Jamaica, June 4–9, 1990, for our Second Encounter. Challenged by the unbearable suffering of the poorest and recapturing the prophetic calling of the Christian faith, we address our sisters and brothers in the churches as well as the peoples of Latin America and the Caribbean to share the experience of this Encounter.

This ecclesiastical event, convened by the Caribbean Conference of Churches, the Antilles Episcopal Conference, the Latin American Council of Churches, and the Ecuadorian Episcopal Conference (Archdiocese of Cuenca), brought together 122 delegates representing 16 different Christian denominations from 33 countries.

Today is the day of Pentecost and, guided by the light of that event, we must liberate ourselves from the prisons of our minds, abandon the temples, and become pilgrims making our way through the cities and countries of our continent. To be with Jesus the Christ is to give testimony to the Risen Lord in the midst of the denial of life to the less fortunate. It is in this spirit that we must build ecumenism centered on the cross as the symbol of the coming together of all churches in response to the cries and suffering of the oppressed.

At the First Encounter held in Cuenca, Ecuador, in November 1986, we reaffirmed the validity of this ecumenical space for reflection, prayer, and sharing of mutual concerns, challenges, and hope. At that First Encounter the following declaration was made:

> The condition of injustice and exploitation that the large majority of the peoples of Latin America and the Caribbean are experiencing results from policies dictated by imperialist Big Power interests, with the collaboration of local power groups. In a special sense this situation is evident at present in the widespread and increasing external debt of Latin America and Caribbean.

This theme of foreign debt identified at that time, combined with that of the drug trade, have been the themes for this 1990 Encounter.

Over the past four years, our peoples have suffered what can no longer be described as a mere deterioration in their environment and in their lives, but a systematic and planned destruction of their health, nutrition, housing, employment, education, and social welfare; a destruction which in almost every country of our region is cloaked by demands for so-called "structural adjustment," designed and imposed by the International Monetary Fund and the World Bank. This creates a state of desperation and anguish at not being able to even begin to find a solution that guarantees a life of human dignity.

The experiences shared at this Encounter by brothers and sisters from different Christian traditions have as their starting point the common experience of commitment to people and the realization that the challenges to the churches come from these same people, the poor and faithful. Over the past week in this ecclesial context, we have lived in Christian fellowship nourished by the Word of God and biblical reflection.

We have examined the themes of the Encounter conscious of the confrontation inherent in the two opposing approaches to them: on the one hand, the logic of capital which places profit before people and, like a new idol, takes a toll of human lives and blood; and on the other hand the logic of life itself inspired by the Gospel, which places supreme value on the human being and encourages us to respect nature and to search for an alternative economic system which guarantees basic human dignity .

Face to face with signs of death such as the deterioration in the condition of life of the majority of our peoples and the transformation of traditional life-giving agricultural practices into profitable industries with the sequel of oppression and death, we see some signs of hope emerging:

- the emergence and strengthening of new social forces such as people's organizations, Christian communities formed by and committed to popular sectors, ethnic nationalities, women's organizations, and ecological movements.

- the feeling of unity and the search for closer integration among the countries of Latin America and the Caribbean.

- the attempts to build for and with the people a new and genuine ethic which struggles against exploitation and injustice and affirms life.

- the prophetic voices and actions of many Christians committed to the development of new, more effective and humane policies.

- the creation of new avenues such as this Encounter for discussion of these problems, which strengthen the ecumenical spirit and facilitate a general level of understanding and the conscientization of the people.

UNDERSTANDING OF THE REALITY
(FOREIGN DEBT AND THE DRUG TRADE)

Foreign Debt and the Drug Trade in Latin America and the Caribbean

Despite the fact that, as far as possible and with painful effort and sacrifice, Latin America and the Caribbean have been complying since 1982 with the agreements regarding foreign debt, it continues to escalate. In fact, between 1982 and 1989 nearly 140 billion dollars have been repaid. However, in this same period foreign debt increased by 140 billion dollars, reaching by the end of 1989 a total of 420 billion dollars. (Some sources say it is far greater.) Hence, for each dollar paid out one more is added to the debt: this is explained by the interest not paid (approximately 50 percent), which is added to the original amount creating a progressive and automatic increase in the total debt, an inexorable process.

Debt repayment is *morally condemnable* because it blindly and brutally undermines the future of humanity itself by fomenting and provoking a catastrophe that destroys human beings and the natural environment in Latin America and the Caribbean. It is therefore evident that payment of the debt is also an ethical question that cannot be based only on the profit motive, but rather on respect for peasants and the life and future of the people. It is for this reason that we dare to assert that debt entrapment is also politically and socially irrational and threatens the very future of the creditors themselves.

Third World debt is today the main lever and mechanism of domination used to maintain the existing "International Economic Order," an unjust order that sustains current imperial domination. There have always been central mechanisms that have sustained bourgeois domination such as colonial occupation and foreign investment. During the past decade, the key mechanism was the foreign debt and its repayment to the point that these are now responsible to a large extent for the affirmation of the imperial system of domination.

The imperialistic system of domination and expansion is set to continue in the Caribbean in 1992 with the planned celebration of the arrival of Columbus and the establishment of a United Europe. We therefore condemn the planned celebration of the beginning of Caribbean colonialism and urge our peoples to observe rather than celebrate 1492. In this observance it will be necessary to review the past in the light of sin and repentance and challenge our peoples not to acquiesce in the celebration of imperialism. Further, we need to educate our people in terms of the implications of a United Europe for the Third World people in their own countries and in the metropolitan countries.

As a result of debt subjugation, we move on from development economies in the 1950s and 1960s to *debt-paying economies,* beginning in 1982. Within this context, all objectives of official political life are subjected to the overriding objective of paying the foreign debt: the structure of production and economic, financial, and social policies. The result is neglect of social policies ("social debt") in vital areas such as heath, education, etc. In this way, loans obtained as "development aid" are recovered now through sacrifices to development. What does this mean? It means that creditor countries hide behind debt repayment in order to hinder the development of underdeveloped countries since these could represent future competitors.

In the free market system based on capital, the debt payment obligations take priority over all other essential human obligations. These latter are therefore considered to be secondary to the priority of payment. It is merely a question of the *logic of the system.* On the other hand, as the effects of debt repayment are hardly discerned and identified as the root of their suffering by those affected, the process of idealization takes advantage of this and even presents it as an ethical obligation.

A *moral question* is being posed, and what is the way of morality? To pay the debt, even though the resulting human suffering is greater than that caused by non-payment? There can be no one answer: it is more ethical and important to satisfy vital needs than to comply with a contract. In this case, the sin would be to comply with the norm to adhere to the law. The sin of which the Christian message speaks is committed when one fulfills the law by going against one's neighbor. It was "in fulfillment of the law" that Jesus was killed! In collecting the debt in the name of an unbreakable law that destroys the human being and the natural environment, creditors are destroying hope and producing despair in our countries. They violate the spirit of God, which consists in "the anticipation of what we shall receive" (Rom. 8:23).

The manipulation of hope is the new dynamic principle of domination, which has been imposed over the last few decades, against what took place in the decades of the 1950s and 1960s, awakening people's hope, economic and social integration for all upon a horizon of dreams. Thus, domination claimed to be the path to the fulfillment of such dreams. But all that ended: the system no longer makes promises, but rather destroys promises and tries to destroy hope. It was discovered that domination has a new thrust based on widespread despair. And the great conclusion: a people that despairs no longer has the capacity to struggle and will no longer be able to build an alternative social program. They will therefore cease to confront domination and exploitation. In this way, the system of domination takes advantage and blackmails in order to convince us that there is no other alternative than its own one. This is the inhumane conclusion that is also drawn up from the present crisis facing the systems of socialism.

The Gospel provides a source and an affirmation of *hope* which is antagonistic to all forces of death. It is a question of hope for life which condemns all sentence of death. This announcement of life defends hope, upon which all human dignity is based. When the system of domination is confronted with the Gospel its stability is endangered. In spite of this, and fully aware of the risks, we condemn debt collection and payment, because it is simply a death sentence upon our peoples and the environment of Latin America and the Caribbean. But it is not only a sentence; it is also a call to all people of good will, especially to the churches and people's organizations. We are called to commit ourselves to life, to denounce all the forces of debt represented by debt payment. This inevitably involves risks. The massacre of the Jesuit priests and their housekeepers in San Salvador on November 16, 1989, conclusively demonstrates this; but it also shows us that in the face of domination and subjection, every effort is worthwhile in promoting the hope of our peoples.

The Drug Trade

Economics and the Drug Trade

During the decade of the 1980s, two phenomena profoundly affected the countries of Latin America and the Caribbean: foreign debt and the drug trade. The drug trade emerged gradually, originating in the Andean countries and spreading to the rest of the Continent in response to the demand for drugs especially from the United States. In a context of economic crisis and recession and the transfer of resources from our countries for debt servicing, the drug trade has had a negative effect on the nations involved and has created a host of far-reaching socio-economic and political problems.

Currently in the Andean Region more than a million persons are directly involved in the production and processing of cocaine. The countries of the Caribbean and some Latin American countries participate in this process as "bridges" for the trans-shipment of the product to the United States and Europe. They also become involved in the economic and financial money laundering networks, further aggravating the problem.

The major part of the resources generated by the drug trade is not reinvested in the producer countries but rather pumped into the financial systems of the metropolitan countries; the case of Jamaica with marijuana and that of the Andean countries with cocaine illustrates the permanent and constant disharmony in all of its economic aspects, legal or illegal. Of the one billion dollars obtained from the drug trade in Jamaica a mere 200 million are reinvested in the country: of the 150 billion dollars (the lowest figure for the cocaine trade exported from the Andean countries), only 8 to 10 billion dollars are ploughed back to the region.

However, and in spite of the ambiguity and contradiction which the above implies, the presence of these resources enables some of our countries to better resist the economic crisis, as they generate employment, inject foreign exchange into the dollar-starved economy, and enable investment to be made in other productive areas — in short, temporarily to cushion the crisis.

Society and the Drug Trade

The process of production of and trading in drugs has enabled the creation of a peasant farming sector in our countries which survives through the cultivation of coca or marijuana and more recently poppy. On the other hand, there is a growing tendency towards domestic consumption, giving rise to the proliferation of small traffickers who, in the economic crisis, carry out this activity as a means of survival. The disintegration of family groups in overcrowded conditions of urban areas and the extreme social injustices which exist contribute to the development of these tendencies.

At the other extreme, drug businesses have emerged — a kind

of "drug elite" which has accumulated power, wealth, and property, which further distort the social processes: new affluent sectors which, as can be seen in the case of Colombia, have caused serious social and political retrogression and the so-called agrarian counter-reform which has led to rural violence.

Crime at the micro-social level, state corruption, and extremely repressive political activities, which violate fundamental human rights, have been some of the consequences of the above. It is, however, in the political arena that the crisis provided by this activity is most clearly manifested.

Politics and the Drug Trade

The state's response has been one of blatant repression, the stepping up of punitive measures and violence against peasant farmers, small traffickers, and consumers without touching the drug lords, with whom it has even cooperated in some instances to neutralize certain leftist groups and people's organizations.

The implementation of repressive legislation against the socially underprivileged has produced the so-called boomerang effect: the problem has not been brought under control but rather has escalated. A problem of economic structure, of poverty and social injustice, is being approached with police repression, even tending currently towards militarization.

This militarization of the conflict is justified rhetorically by the fact that the drug trade has posed major challenges to the stability of various countries, on the one hand, and because of pressure from the United States on the other. Nevertheless, the remedy seems to be worse than the disease, in that basic human rights are abrogated. There is a rise in authoritarianism and a breakdown of the state apparatus. Moreover, this has led to corruption in the armed forces, as can be seen in several cases. Civilian governments are not immune to these corrupting influences either, as manifested in the administration of justice, in political parties, and even at the highest level of government. Therefore, by declaring war against growing sectors of the population, the state undermines its own legitimacy, political institutions become corrupted, and repression escalates.

International Relations and the Drug Trade

All these policies are not derived from a Latin American and Caribbean diagnosis of the problem but from the United States approach to the topic. For this reason, the economic, social, and political cost of drugs is being borne by our countries.

The contradiction in United States policies is obvious: There is no control of the laundering of dollars in American banks. Neither is the trade in those elements used in refining drugs nor the trade in arms by the drug lords. U.S. policy, based as it is on the doctrine of "national security," has violated our sovereignty, as we have seen in the case of the invasion of Panama; it has heightened violence and militarization in our societies under the pretext of combating the drug trade in the Andean and Caribbean regions, and not yet on the streets of New York, Los Angeles, and Miami. This has engendered social insecurity in our countries.

We are once again faced with the imposition of unilateral policies and ideas whereby one country determines what the others should do without taking into account their problems and real needs. In our case, these are our development, our foreign debt, the economic trade imbalance, the search for solutions to social inequalities, and people's participation in the exercise of power.

Therefore, we need a new focus whereby the drug problem is tackled along with all the other problems in an effort to find solutions. Such solutions should not promote social and political violence. Neither should they approach the problem in terms of a "war" in which the battlefield is our countries; rather, it should encourage multilateral and concerted action and not interference by an extra-regional hegemonic power.

Considerations for Our Churches

In order to achieve the above, there is a need for a change in our perception. The issue must be removed from the realm of ideology, and the cooperation of important social influences such as the churches should be enlisted in order to diffuse violence and facilitate the just solution of a problem which affects millions of Caribbean and Latin American peoples. The churches can help in clarifying the problem of the drug trade as over against the planting and use of the coca leaf, which is a traditional practice among the peasant communities of the Andean Region and offers a service both to their health and cultural identity.

In this respect, the Christian churches, in conjunction with other sectors (teachers, people's organizations, etc.) can contribute to achieving a shift in perspective, away from confrontation to dialogue. To make this change possible, the churches need to be self-critical as they have neither reflected seriously nor interpreted and given Gospel responses to the problem, recapturing the Christian understanding of life over against the alienation caused by the drug problem.

It is not through military wars and low-intensity conflicts that the drug problem will be solved, nor will we make any progress in this respect through guerilla warfare and violence. Since the drug trade has been caused by the economic crisis and by the abject poverty of vast sectors of the population, the solution should be linked to long-term policies in which Latin America and the Caribbean must have an input through dialogue or consensus. We cannot even think of ending the drug trade without first focusing on changing the unjust structures at the social, economic, and political levels from the point of view of the Christian commitment to the poor, the marginalized, and downtrodden who are the real victims of the war against drugs.

ENLIGHTENMENT OF FAITH

Idolatry, the Main Sin of Affluent Societies

This reality, insofar as it involves exploitation of the human person, oppression of the poor and powerless, contempt for human dignity, injustice and lack of solidarity, runs counter to God's plan. The root cause of all this is human selfishness – the disavowing of one's neighbor. From the point of view of faith, this is called sin. We can speak of a mystery of sin and a mystery of iniquity. We are placed in a situation of systemic acts of sin which springs from within ourselves and is introduced in each of us through selfishness. Sin is both personal and social, given that personal sin is enmeshed in structures, creating an atmosphere of collective sin. When sin permeates social structures and corrupts the people's attitudes and conduct, the atmosphere becomes polluted and is transformed into the incarnation of evil and wicked forces (see Eph. 6:12).

At the root of our system, idolatry is seen to be the worst sin: the idolatry of possession, power, and pleasure at the expense of human beings. Through idolatry the person is subordinated to things. Objects are erected as truly enslaving idols whose main victims are the poor and those who struggle for the cause of justice. "No one can be a slave of two masters," said Jesus on one occasion (Matt. 6:24). For his part, the Apostle Paul warns us that greed is a form of idolatry (see Col. 3:5). Similarly, power which is imposed on others and violates their rights is a form of idolatry, and so also is unfettered consumerism which allows squandering by the privileged minority, while for the vast majority not even basic necessities can be met. The underdeveloped condition of some peoples and the extremely high levels of development of others are both inhuman conditions which are interrelated and reveal a state of sin based on injustice and apathy.

The wrath of God is directed against those empires erected at the expense of other nations. "Howl in pain! The day of the Lord is near, the day when the Almighty brings destruction" (Isa. 13:8). God puts himself on the side of the powerless: "I have indeed heard the cry of my people, and I see how Egyptians are oppressing them" (Exod. 3:9). It seems that the prophecy of Habakkuk is today being fulfilled: "You have cut down the forests of Lebanon; now you will be cut down. You killed its animals; now animals will terrify you. This will happen because of the murders you have committed and because of your violence against the people of the world and its cities" (Hab. 2:17).

The God of Jesus Christ, the Hope and Strength of the Poor

In Jesus' redeeming work, salvation is always possible (see Luke 4:18-20). We must affirm with conviction the possibility and confidence in salvation based on the divine promise, by virtue of which contemporary history is not locked into itself, but open to the Kingdom of God. This faith and hope is based on the power of God who "chose what the world considers nonsense in order to shame the wise, and he chose what the world considers weak in order to shame the powerful" (1 Cor. 1:27).

The option for the poor who have built our churches is the expression of loyalty to God who said blessed are the poor (see Luke 6:20), who first preached his Gospel to them (see Matt. 11:5), and who will judge us by our response to their needs (see Matt. 25:31-46).

Faced with the egoism and individualism characteristic of large-sized private property, Christians considered all goods they possessed as common property (see Acts 4:32-37). This same spirit is found today in so many Christian communities and mass organizations that look for ways to meet the bare necessities of life by the practice of sharing.

Our trust in the Lord sustains us and gives us hope, for he is with us always, to the end of the age (see Matt. 29:20). He promised us his Holy Spirit to give us guidance, comfort, and succor: "I will ask the Father, and he will give you another Helper, who will stay with you forever. He is the Spirit, who reveals the truth about God. The world cannot receive him, because it cannot see him or know him. But you know him, because he remains with you and is in you" (John 14:16-17).

The Defense of Life, the Basis for Christian Ethics

The dignity of each individual as being made in Christ's image must inspire Christian action in the world. The awareness of a common Father in God and of the fellowship in Christ ascribes to our world outlook new criteria for interpreting it and for seeking avenues of justice and social change.

From the very beginning of time, the need has existed to create a social and economic order with the human person as first, last, and center of all society. This new order, similarly, needs to inspire relations between countries, solidarity and brotherhood being based on ethical requirements and Christian principles of justice. Relationships between people and between nations ought to be grounded in service and not in the all-consuming and complete craving for wealth or acquisitions.

The unpayable debt symbolizes total dependence and enslavement. There is an old adage which says: "One does not owe what one cannot pay." In order to ask God's forgiveness for our sins and misdeeds, we must ourselves be prepared to forgive all the wrongs done to us (see Luke 11:4). On the basis of this principle of forgiveness and love of God, we ought to identify the solution to the unbearable and inhuman condition of debt entrapment. What comes into play, in the first place, is not the balance on the accounts of the international creditors, but the lives of millions of people who can no longer bear the permanent threat of economic prescriptions which bring in their wake unemployment, misery, and death. Such policies trample on the dignity of humanity, the defense and support of which have been entrusted to us by the Creator.

Christ, who did not come to supersede the law but rather to give it definite shape (see Matt. 5:17), proposes a new form of justice based on the respect for the human being beyond any laws and even religious traditions: "The Sabbath was made for the good of man; man was not made for the Sabbath" (Mark 2:27). When the fulfillment of any norm, legitimate though it may be, is accomplished at the cost of human lives, it becomes a source of sin. This is so in the case of the payment of the foreign debt, which brings with it destruction and death due to the greed of its creditors.

Within the principle of respect for life we must consider the problem of the drug trade, looking not only at the lives of those who destroy themselves through the consumption of drugs, but also at those who, in order to survive, must accept work which involves, in spite of themselves, an illicit and corrupt trade. This situation, which has resulted in the current crisis, must be faced, recognizing the right of every human being to dignified and well-paid work and the right of our peoples to search for and decide on the solutions to their problems, within a spirit of dialogue, cooperation, and solidarity, and not through the imposition of foreign domination.

The problems of foreign debt and drug trade, on a global level, are not reducible to problems merely of an economic or political nature, but are ethical as well, and will need to be raised and resolved, since they assume sinful structures which, in turn, affect human lives. Faith demands of us personal conversion and commitment to structural change. Without personal conversion, the change of structures merely gives way to the forms of oppression and alienation of persons. Without commitment to bring about this change in structures, conversion gets lost in disembodied spiritualism.

We bring this Encounter to a close by examining the main challenges raised by the themes discussed and by making our commitments, hoping in this way to contribute to the evangelizing mission of the church in the world.

Christian Spirituality

The challenges which surfaced over the period and the fraternal spirit pervading the Encounter have led us to reaffirm some of the pillars of our Christian spirituality or mystique. These constitute the basis of our contribution to the transformation of this world from the holistic standpoint envisaged by the Kingdom of God.

We affirm faith in the resurrection of the Lord Jesus, faith which sustains hope and guarantees final victory over idolatry and enslavement.

We take on a preferential option for the poor and marginalized, recognizing their leading role in the proclamation of the Kingdom of God and in the building of a just, egalitarian, and fraternal society.

Sincerely acknowledging our shortcomings, we affirm the need for deep conversion which implies the giving up of manipulative practices and domination, beginning to live the spirit of service according to the Gospel.

Our Judgments in the Face of the Facts as Presented

We reject the prevailing ideology in both the developed and underdeveloped countries which leads to the acceptance of existing inequalities as the basis of development.

We reject the domination being exercised in our countries by the introduction of the free market system, since it is a representation of the law of the mighty over the weak, and declare the need to create an alternative international economic order, which has as its priority the satisfaction of all of the basic needs of every individual.

We condemn those statements and practices which, masquerading under the cloak of morality, are in fact attacks against the identity of our people, and constitute a war which destroys human lives and violates the sovereignty of our countries.

We place a high value on human life, in particular the lives of the poor (the farmers, the indigenous populations, and the depressed sectors), and we place emphasis on the value of their cultures and mores; these sectors have been misunderstood and even treated as "scapegoats" for the excesses and deviant behavior of modern culture.

We defend every life form, not merely the life of individuals and peoples but also the value of the natural environment, which has to be respected and preserved for the benefit of all humankind.

We reject those policies and organizations such as the International Monetary Fund and the World Bank as well as the private commercial banking sector which generate poverty in the Third World through their loan management and debt collection. These show no consideration for the supreme right of individuals and countries to a dignified existence, to sustainable development.

In the context of the Andean peoples and their traditions, we submit that the indigenous populations have a right to cultivate the coca crop, and we believe that this practice is a gift from God through the Pachamama (Mother Earth) and a source of health and life for them.

Moreover, we denounce all attempts to consider the use of the coca leaf by the local population as a form of escape or abnormality in the human being. Likewise, we reject all attempts to link the problem of drug addiction and cocaine trade to this practice. For these attempts are merely to justify repression as a means of maintaining a hold over our people.

In all of these issues, we find the scourge of racism ever present. It oppresses and marginalizes people of African descent as well as indigenous populations and migrant minorities who are the ones that suffer most from the consequences of the policies of multilateral organizations and powerful nations.

We painfully acknowledge the condition of the majority of children of Latin America and the Caribbean who are the main victims of the problems examined, and we call on the church in the name of the God of life to ensure that their right to a decent human life is recognized and respected.

Call to the Churches

We must work and reflect more intensely on the Word of God, recapturing the primordial character of Christian hope as a means of overcoming the frustration and despair of many of our brothers and sisters.

As Christians we reaffirm the prophetic mission of the church, generating new thinking and theological discussion capable of questioning positions, structures, and dominant ideas and of calling for and stimulating a life of solidarity with the masses.

Our churches are engaged in very serious efforts to live out our option for the poor and are taking many risks. Moreover, we recognize that the poor in Latin America and the Caribbean are often marginalized from the work of the church and do not participate in it. Furthermore, we are also aware that, in practice, the churches often become insensitive to the needs of the people and continue to maintain authoritarian and chauvinistic attitudes.

Recognizing that the churches do not play the dominant role in building a new society, we support the role of people's organizations and other groups which join in the struggle for human dignity and vital social change, by establishing an ongoing and fruitful dialogue with them.

We see the need for a ministry of solidarity and support, in taking a stance with all the victims of foreign debt, the drug trade, and coca cultivation.

We also think it necessary to begin a process of study and reflection on the topics of this Encounter, which would not be confined to the elite but would extend to all the members of our communities. The study would include the question of the decriminalization of drug abuse as well as other social and ethical problems which also need clarification.

We must reaffirm and update the Christian doctrine regarding usury in light of the scourge which debt repayment represents. And in this regard, we reject the added temptation to churches to participate in debt purchase.

We also reaffirm the primacy of human life over the pursuit of wealth and of justice over gain, while defending the right of the poor to participate equally in the distribution of wealth.

Our churches must bring pressure to bear upon multilateral lending agencies, private banks, and influential persons so that they might give themselves to the establishment of a just international economic order as a viable alternative to the present order.

We must carry out our commitment to bring about change in our churches, and in this way contribute to the elimination of injustice and inhumanity in Latin American and Caribbean societies.

We must especially undertake an education program, disseminating required information to pastors, leaders, and lay members of the churches.

Finally, we emphasize the importance of ecumenism and the need to strengthen it based on an option for the poor and in the creation of the church of the poor – an ecumenism that is capable of presenting a united front to protect the gift of life.

We commit ourselves to establishing national or regional ecumenical commissions, which will study the subject of socioeconomic and political solutions to the themes dealt with here.

9

Women in the Caribbean

WOMEN IN THE STRUGGLE
by Joan French

The Caribbean has had a long history of slavery and colonialism. These dark hours of our history were marked by genocide (the near extermination of indigenous peoples) and the brutality of forced labor of African peoples under slavery and Asian peoples under the indentureship system. The monopoly of the best material resources by whites, the favored position of "brown" people as compared to the black population, and the violence used to prevent the equitable access of the black population to economic, social, and political power have left behind a society scarred by racism and bitter class struggle.

Nevertheless, the struggles of Caribbean people against this oppression and exploitation have been as glorious as the attempts at marginalization have been unrelenting. Ostracism and martyrdom have been the price paid by the bold.

In all the stages of these struggles women have been present. However, the patriarchal structures imposed on the society influenced the writing of history, even that history that recorded the challenge to injustice. The political movements which opposed colonialism were also dominated by males. Until recently little was known about the role of women in these struggles: indeed, it was often assumed that they had none.

The emergence of a new wave of feminist activity in the Caribbean in the 1970s led to a re-examination of history and to startling discoveries about the role and level of political action by women

Joan French, a Jamaican, is director of the Caribbean Policy Development Centre. A daughter organization of the Caribbean Conference of Churches, the CPDC coordinates the development work of the NGOs in the region.

under slavery, in the black nationalist movements of the turn of the century and beyond, in the massive region-wide rebellions of the 1930s, in the struggles for political independence in the 1950s and 1960s. Nevertheless, the emerging feminist movement of the 1970s had to contend with continuing subordination of gender issues in the black power movement and socialism which flowered in the late 1960s and early 1970s. Throughout the later 1970s and the 1980s these forces continued to contend, until today, with the difference that today a focus on gender analysis and feminist issues is generally considered respectable at the level of intellectual discourse, even if the divergence from actual practice often remains marked.

This new wave of feminist activity in the Caribbean sought not only to challenge the subordinate nature of women's insertion into the social structure in relation to men, but to confront issues of race, class, and imperialism from a gender perspective, to seek innovative forms of organizing and political action to replace the power hierarchy and psychological and physical violence of patriarchal institutions and structures. It sought to recognize and challenge divisions of race, class, and gender, and to deepen the analysis of these divisions in search of more meaningful democratic processes. It explored the private areas of women's lives in order to make their hidden concerns visible.

In the course of this challenge women organized around a range of issues including:

- a new definition of work to include women's unpaid domestic labor
- exploitation of women's domestic labor
- rights of women workers in and out of the home
- recognition of women's reproductive labor and its social role
- equitable access of women to material resources including wages
- social stereotyping of women and men
- the role of spirituality and creativity in human development
- women's reproductive health and sexual rights
- violence against women
- legal reform to support the rights of women

- The super-exploitation of women's labor, the undermining of women's social supports, and the recolonization of Caribbean society and the deepening of dependency under the structural adjustment policies of the International Monetary Fund, the World Bank, and fraternal institutions.

RELIGIOUS ISSUES
by Ruth Anne Goldson

The following issues were identified at an ecumenical conference to prepare for the Ecumenical Decade of Churches in Solidarity with Women. They were further discussed and amplified in discussion with the coordinating committee for the ecumenical "Women in Ministries" program being undertaken in association with the Caribbean Conference of Churches.

1. Participation of Women in the Church

a. Need to seek to realize the biblical mandate for men and women in *partnership* in the church and the building of an inclusive community.

b. Concern that many churches are comprised of mainly women and children and that the men are not active as regular worshippers but mainly in leadership positions.

c. Need for clarification and definition of the roles that women play in the various churches. Where are the women and what is the level of integration and participation at all levels of the church?

d. Need to explore the avenues for education and training for women in church ministries and to evaluate the effectiveness of the training.

e. Need to develop and strengthen support systems for women in ordained and specialized ministries.

f. Need to identify contribution made by women in the church and to highlight this contribution so as to encourage other women.

Ruth Anne Goldson is a Moravian pastor from Barbados.

2. Health, Reproduction, Nutrition, Sexuality, Identity

a. The question of reproduction, especially the right of control and choice.

b. Recognition of the increasing contribution being made by church clinics and the need to explore ways of facilitating the range of services, e.g., family, vocational, and general counselling.

3. Family Life Education

a. Need for consideration of gender issues.

b. The problem of violence and incest in the family and society.

c. The need for continuing family life education especially in areas such as parenting skills for single mothers and parents with adolescent children.

d. Concern for the absence of positive male role models in the family in view of the large number of women who are heads of households. The need for the church to support women in this situation but recognition of the difficulties as many congregations are predominantly female.

4. Economic Issues Particularly Impacting on Women

a. Institutional prostitution, particularly that linked to tourism.

b. The high proportion of households headed by women and their ability to cope given economic recession in the countries of the region. The need for the church to participate actively in development programs seeking to empower the women.

c. The problem of dependency. Many women are solely dependent on economic support from their male partners. This often places them at great disadvantage especially in cases of violence and other abuse in the home.

d. The low status and low pay assigned to work done by women. The need for the church to increase its advocacy on behalf of women working and living under subhuman conditions in the home and at the workplace.

10

Pastoral Testimony

An Interview with Raúl Suárez

There follows an interview between Carmelo Alvarez, executive director of DEI (Departamento Ecuménico de Investigaciones) in San José, Costa Rica, and Rev. Raúl Suárez, pastor of the Baptist Church in Marianao, Cuba, and chairman of the Ecumenical Council of Cuba.The interview was translated by Stella Mastrangelo.

Carmelo: *Raúl, in the first place I would like to know what your roots are, where in Cuba you come from, what your family background is.*

Raúl: I come from a family of agricultural workers, which in our capitalistic past was one of the poorest sectors, perhaps the most exploited by our sugar barons. My family consisted of my parents, five sisters, and four brothers. Usually, my father was the only one who worked. The work lasted three and a half to four months a year, during the sugar cane harvest. The rest of the year was slack time, what in Cuba was called "dead time." The poor families had to go out in the woods to make charcoal in order to survive. For this reason, the children of these families had to leave school early. When the revolution came, the only one in my family who could read and write was me. My own level was a little higher because in 1956 I had encountered the Gospel, and then I felt the need to be prepared.

Carmelo: *Meeting the Gospel made you feel the need to be trained, and you think this motivated you to study?*

Raúl: Because of the poverty in which our family lived, all of us had to work. By the time I was nine or ten I was doing errands for middle-class families. My sisters were employed as house servants for a dismal salary. When I turned eighteen I left home, being practically illiterate. I met the Gospel in a very dramatic way, because it was after a twenty-four-hour drinking spell, as I was sleeping out on the street in a Matanzas neighborhood. I awoke and had an experience that made me feel the need to change the way I lived and, above all, the need to get rid of the thing I wanted to drown in alcohol, the past that surfaced in dreams and nightmares. I called to God from the bottom of my heart to change my life. I had an experience of the faith that led to a total break with my old way of living and understanding life. I went back to my home town and joined the Baptist church. Being illiterate, I asked the pastor to help me. He and his wife helped me to do an almost unbelievable thing: to study the eight years of elementary school in order to enter the seminary a year and a half later. Thank God, the Gospel for me meant a wish to educate myself in order to be socially useful. Then I oriented my life toward the Christian ministry within the Baptist denomination.

I contacted a humble workers' church, which did a great deal of good for me. Two years after receiving the Gospel I entered the Baptist seminary in Havana. That meant entering a new relationship. As I came in contact with this religious world of the seminary and the ministry, I gradually experienced a loss of my class consciousness. Without noticing it, my mentality was becoming middle class. I was trying to imitate the role of the doctor, the priest, the lawyer, the attorney, even in the way I dressed. On the weekends, when I preached, I always had to wear a suit. Now I have a problem with my size. I have never been able to find clothes right for me; I always have to get them fixed. At that time I rolled my trousers up, because they were too long for me. Today I laugh about that. To my people I looked like a scarecrow. Without realizing it, I was losing contact with my roots, I was denying them. To some degree, I was betraying my class.

As a child, I felt a deep social concern. I rebelled against my people's situation, the exploitation my father suffered. I was even something of an atheist, due to the fact that the owner of the *hacienda* where my father worked was the chairman of Catholic Action in our town. He exploited my father from Monday to Saturday and then on Sundays, while my father had to go on working on his land, he was at the Catholic church wearing a

fine straw hat, an expensive linen suit, and two-tone shoes. I felt
hatred against the Catholic religion, and against religion of any
kind.

I made contact with the people at Ciénega de Zapata, which is
a very poor place, the poorest people in the whole country. After
the impact of the revolution, I had to decide between staying here
or going to Ciénega de Zapata.

One day, as I was praying, I heard a voice saying to me, in my
conscience: "Why don't you go to Ciénega de Zapata?" So, I decided
to start again living among the peasants, where I had to live in a
hut with a dirt floor, wooden walls, and a mud roof. There I had
my second conversion. I felt the need to beg God never to let me
forget my social origins.

At the time I felt a deep conflict. I felt an extraordinary sympathy for Fidel and the others, I felt loyalty to my origins, and I
saw the transformations the revolution was bringing about. But this
revolution was taking a communist path. How could I, being a Christian, cooperate with an atheistic system? That is what I kept asking
myself.

Carmelo: *And how did you solve that dilemma?*

Raúl: I listened to Fidel and was moved by his speeches. But I
rejected his communism. I rejected the communist orientation the
revolution had taken.

Then I came into contact with some different literature that I
ordered from the Matanzas seminary. I read theologians like Barth,
Tillich, and Brunner whom I had not studied at the seminary. They
helped me see certain things.

But what helped me most was the fact that the revolution was
helping the people. One would have to be blind not to see what
was being done in the fields of education and health. One of my
younger brothers had died for lack of medical assistance. How could
I not see? I saw hospitals and schools being built. The achievements
of the revolution were an overwhelming fact!

Another factor that carried great weight for me was that since
1955 I had sympathized with what was happening in the United
States around the figure of Martin Luther King. He was a Baptist
minister. With elements from Gandhi and Thoreau, yes, but he was a
man who drank from the Bible, especially the New Testament. That
was where his sermons came from. Martin Luther King's personality

made me feel a deep affection for him, for his writings and his work. The day he was killed I cried like a little child.

My present convictions owe much to my children. My children did not know capitalism: they were born in the revolution. It is my children who question the most my pastoral approach and my theological perspective. It is they who have always demanded transparency in my acts and in my motivations. They want consistency in what I believe and what I think.

The Marxist critique of religion has not hurt us; on the contrary, it has helped us. What hurts the Christian faith is the mellowing out, the softening it undergoes in capitalistic society in order to make it fit into that society. The Marxist critique of religion has helped me to get rid of the ideological shell. In this sense my encounter with Marxism has been at the same time the encounter with a new reading of the Bible, and of our liturgy, and of the history of Cuba, and of the history of Baptists in Cuba. Today I love the Bible more. It is now, Carmelo, that the Bible is the rule of faith and practice for us. And it is the true source that shapes our convictions, and not as it was before, which was the opposite: we brought to the Bible all our certainties and our ways to live and understand our faith, and we imposed all that ideological load on it.

Carmelo: *The Raúl Suárez who has said all this is above all a pastor, a pastor who criticizes his Baptist tradition but stays within it, a Baptist pastor who does theology from within this perspective and incorporates the socialist context in which he lives, and who goes to the sources of this socialism, and obviously also goes to the sources of theology. How does this Baptist pastor manage in Cuba today? What is his life project as a local church pastor?*

Raúl: You have touched upon the fact that in spite of the contradictions we have had at the Baptist Convention, we remain Baptists. We plan to end as such. Independently of any sectarian idea, we are convinced that if there is one church that in its historical process, in its origins, has the elements to live creatively and happily in a socialist system, it is our Baptist tradition. When Baptists began, their pastors were elected by the people, their system was democratic. Now, in a process like ours, these roots are only enriched. That is why we feel well within our Baptist tradition and we want to be loyal to it, and not heed the distortions that may crop up at a specific moment. We are in love with our church.

The fact that as a pastor you visit people in hospitals, you visit the sick, you have to meet death, the doubts raised by life itself, the problems of the young and the children, the difficulties they face still today in relating to their school principals, all that helps us not to forget that we are part of a community, not an elitist organization severed from that human basis. This relationship helps me, because there is the danger of thinking of the church as an institution, an impersonal entity. When you are a pastor, you realize the church is Lorenza, Juana, Pedro, human beings. Children, old persons, the young. That there are problems, joy, hope, and also suffering and death. That is life. It is the same thing Fidel has told the party, that they have to be in touch with the masses. I think that we, ecumenical and Christian leaders, must have tight links with one community, feel part of it.

Carmelo: *Another subject I want to go into is your ecumenical experience, which is also a different view of your pastoral activity and your commitment in Cuba. You are the chairman of the Cuban Ecumenical Committee. You have been executive secretary of the same committee and have represented Cuba in international gatherings.*

Raúl: Something I noticed from the start in the ecumenical movement, not only here but in other places too, is that ecumenism can be merely a church leaders' thing, without involving their churches. There is a "personalities ecumenism," which works around ecumenism without much of a social basis.

Not long ago I was telling the general secretary of the World Council of Churches that we must eliminate this kind of ecumenism that sometimes develops in our towns, which is an ecumenism-between-friends, so to speak, a partners' ecumenism. Sometimes, people from Geneva or from Germany invite their friends here, and their friends here in turn invite their friends there to come visit Cuba. That is a friendly exchange that enriches their friendship, but it does not reach our people. They do not feel any need to inform the others, and as their travels are not related to any global ecumenical project but to the relationships they have formed, all their goings and comings do not have any consequences for a national ecumenism. That does not do any good.

Carmelo: *Raúl, I am deeply grateful for this dialogue. Really, the richness of your passionate message, with your deep Christian and revolutionary conviction, helps us to put into perspective the richness and the challenge that life in the church and in the Cuban revolution represent for us.*

Raúl: I want to sum up what I have been trying to say in this interview. After twenty-nine years spent in the Cuban revolutionary process, and the twenty-two years I lived prior to that in the capitalistic system, I feel in my heart the urge to renew the triple petition I have always addressed to God: May I never forget where I come from, my social origins. May I never forget that when I was illiterate and a victim of vice, when my life had no meaning, Christ came to me and gave it a meaning. May I never forget that this revolution of ours, with its many achievements, and with its errors too, also gave meaning to my pastoral work and to my Christian ministry. All this leads me to say what I always say to God in my prayers, and to our church: I have no words sufficient to thank God for having lived these twenty-nine years together with our people, so heroic and courageous, so humble and yet so great.

11

Continental Encounter for the Pastoral Accompaniment of the Churches and the People of Cuba

We, representatives of the Canadian Council of Churches, the National Council of Churches of Christ in the USA, the Caribbean Conference of Churches, the Latin American Council of Churches, and the Ecumenical Council of Cuba, have met in the City of Havana, from the 9th to the 12th of December of 1991, Year of our Lord, in the Continental Encounter for the Pastoral Accompaniment of the Churches and the People of Cuba.

We have arrived at a difficult time in our history, a result of the process of aggression against Cuba by the successive administrations of the United States, expressed by the blockade, which has to be rejected morally and theologically. This blockade not only isolates Cuba from the rest of the world, but also asphyxiates the Cuban people, trying to bend their spirit of self-determination. Another factor involved in the present crisis is the collapse of the socialist system in Eastern and Central Europe, resulting in Cuba's economic isolation.

For more than thirty years, the length of the revolutionary process, there have been several exchanges between the churches and ecumenical organizations from abroad and the churches and ecumenical organizations of Cuba, all of which have confirmed their solidarity with the people of Cuba. At this time in Cuba, we have come to accompany the people and the Cuban churches, fellow-partners sharing bread, that is life, in the struggle for justice and hope.

This commitment of walking together with the churches and the people of Cuba has come out of obedience to the evangelical proclamation of the Kingdom, in the sense in which Saint Luke announced it: "The Kingdom of God does not come with your careful observation, nor will people say, 'here it is,' or 'There it is,' because the kingdom of God is within you" (Luke 17:20–21 NIV).

The Christian faith cannot in any way be interpreted as a political system or an ideology, but, because of its profound commitment to life, to love, to peace, and to justice, it defies the structures of power and the ideologies that do not value life and promote death; that do not love the neighbor, but reject him/her, that practice war and injustice as a method and a system to achieve at any cost egocentric goals.

In a world of oppression, injustice, and death the evangelical proclamation of a more just and human kingdom, as a hope and a possibility, makes the powers of darkness and of death feel threatened and insecure.

The kingdom, as a promise of life after death, does not frighten the powerful; instead they themselves preach a future consolation for the poor who live in injustice. What really does frighten the powerful is the gradual coming into view of the signs of the kingdom, which are not utopia but real possibilities, like love and justice among human beings. That is why they try to falsify them.

Starting from our evangelical vision of life is born our commitment in favor of those signs of the kingdom that we perceive in the struggle of the Christians and the people of Cuba in favor of life. This stimulates us to a mutual accompaniment of the churches and the Cuban people.

In view of this we have agreed to develop a wide scope of actions on the part of the churches in Cuba, the continent, and the Caribbean, beginning with continuous prayers in our communities and parishes.

We have committed ourselves to fulfill joint prophetic actions, in the search for truth and justice, in the fields of theology, diplomacy, economy, and politics.

We commit ourselves to work, in short, medium, and long terms, according to the priorities:

- To achieve the total lifting of the blockade of the United States against Cuba.

- To provide humanitarian help, especially medicine and food for children, women, and elderly people who are suffering the impact of the blockade.

- To promote an exchange at the people-to-people level between Cuba, Latin America, Canada, and the United States of America, in different sectors, i.e., grassroots groups, women, youth, etc.

- To establish alternative networks of information to educate our people in relation to the Cuban reality.

- To commit ourselves, both the Christians in Cuba and the continent, to deepen the dialogue ecumenically with other Christians (Evangelicals and Roman Catholics), so that our witness in favor of life will be an expression of the unity of church.

- To stimulate the churches in Cuba and abroad to recognize the unity of the Cuban people, in the spirit of reconciliation, as a necessary element to conquer the difficulties that have come up in these times of crisis, and that unity shall include the Cuban community abroad.

Guided by the power of the Holy Spirit, we want to assume this commitment of accompanying the sisters and brothers of the churches in Cuba, in their responsibility of being and walking together with their people in this special time, in order to protect life and human dignity.

12

Caribbean Ecumenism
and Emancipation Theology

by Adolfo Ham

As we have seen in previous chapters, Caribbean society was determined very much by an economy of slavery. However, around 1830, the process of emancipation from slavery started in the English Caribbean up to Cuba, which was the last island in the Caribbean to eliminate slavery. Several social scientists and theologians have stated that both the "plantation mentality" and the "slavery mentality" have had tremendous effects on the Caribbean soul up to the present time. So we can ask ourselves what were the effects in our societies as a whole. Kortright Davis, an Anglican priest from Antigua who is professor of theology at Howard University's School of Theology, says rightly that "emancipation is for Caribbean people a strong emotive word, connoting that spirituality of freedom which they are pursuing." (That is why he prefers to speak of a "theology of emancipation" for the region more than a "liberation theology"). He asks these searching questions:

> What is it in the Caribbean experience that still hinders the process of full emancipation? Is there not a need to dig deep into our own historical consciousness and to reapply ourselves to the task that was arrested or deferred somewhere along the line? Is it not true that the most crucial human need in the Caribbean at this time is neither trade, nor aid, nor arms, nor even the liberation of the mind, but rather the emancipation of the *disvalued self?*[1]

Adolfo Ham, a native of Cuba, is the Regional Programme Co-ordinator, Theological Reflection & Conscientization, Caribbean Conference of Churches.

1. Kortright Davis, *Emancipation Still Comin'* (Maryknoll, N.Y.: Orbis, 1990), 103.

Closely related with emancipation is the process of decolonization and independence of the region's territories. The Rev. Ashley Smith, president of the United Church of Jamaica and the Grand Cayman Reformed Churches, ponders: "One of the demands of genuine independence is that we take final responsibility for determining what needs to be done, the order in which our priorities must come, and the strategies for addressing the goals which we set for ourselves."[2]

As we have been commemorating in the Caribbean as well as in the rest of the Americas the quincentennial of Columbus's arrival, we have to reflect seriously on all that that has meant for our people in terms of the genocide of the native population and the wiping out of their culture, their replacement with enslaved workers from Africa and, later on, indentured workers from Asia.

The Rev. William Watty, a Methodist minister from Dominica who is now in Antigua serving as president of the Methodist Church in the Caribbean and the Americas, wrote in 1973, "What Europe and America (the USA) have gained because of colonization can perhaps be reckoned by economic historians, but what the world has lost because of the interruption of the histories of other peoples and the callous destruction of other cultures is beyond human computation."[3]

The Trinidadian Idris Hamid, whose untimely death in August 1981 deprived the Caribbean of one of its main theologians, spoke frequently about the "decolonization of theology."[4] Hamid said that since colonization took place on at least four levels — political, economic, cultural, and religious — the "decolonization" of theology has also to refer to these four dimensions. If bad theology had been used during the time of the colony for the justification of oppression or the conditioning of the people for domination, good theology now had "to work for the recovery of the Caribbean man/woman.... The new Caribbean person is not only an individual, but it is a community."[5]

---

2. Ashley Smith, *Real Roots and Potted Plants* (Eureka: Mandeville, 1984), 59.

3. Rev. William Watty, in *The Troubling of the Waters,* ed. Idris Hamid (San Fernando, Trinidad, 1973), 74.

4. Idris Hamid, *In Search of New Perspectives* (Barbados: CADEC, 1971), 12.

5. Idris Hamid, *With Eyes Wide Open* (Kingston: CADEC, 1973).

Elements for a Caribbean Theology

William Watty says "theology is a superfluous element in human thought unless it provides a people where they are with a perspective and a self-evaluation which is both authentic and inspiring."[6]

In the Bible we do not seek for an oracle. We like to look for what it speaks for us *here* and *now*. We like a "political reading": What does it say about liberation in the Caribbean? How can it empower the poor and marginalized? What does it say about power? Why is God always siding with the poor and the oppressed? That is the reason we practice a "popular reading" of the Bible: How many beautiful and inspiring insights the poor discover in the Bible without the technical tools for interpretation!

We have to start with the doctrine of God. Idris Hamid says: "Not only has God had to go underground in Caribbean history, but Caribbean man had to take his survival kit there, too. All his creativity and cultural forms which were subjected to official abuse found a home." We have to analyze the extent to which God himself has been misrepresented or "colonized."[7]

The Christian church is "the bearer of identity," says Noel L. Erskine, the Jamaican Baptist presently teaching at Candler School of Theology in Atlanta.[8] The church has assumed three attitudes: a church that has maintained the status quo to the extent of compromising its message; a church *for* the people, an agent of socialization, looking down to the poor, being part of the ruling class; and a church *of* the people, "the home of God's people," in which the Christian community sees itself as the vanguard of the people. In some places the experience of "base ecclesial communities" has contributed to the renewal of Caribbean ecclesiology. But we have to acknowledge the fact that much of the survival of the Caribbean people and their culture, much of the development of their self-identity and self-respect, have been preserved by and in the church.

This takes us to the question of the relation between gospel and culture. Kortright Davis points to four negative elements in the Caribbean reality that affect very much the quality of life: poverty,

---

6. Watty, "The Troubling of the Waters," 79.
7. Idris Hamid, *With Eyes Wide Open,* 125.
8. Noel L. Erskine, *Decolonizing Theology — A Caribbean Perspective* (Maryknoll, N.Y.: Orbis Books, 1981), 81.

versus the efforts by NGOs and churches to find a holistic approach
to development; the political problem of dependence, the "neocolonial syndrome" closely related to poverty, versus the faith, hope,
and courage to assert one's self-determination; cultural alienation as
a result of the assault of the powerful U.S. electronic media, versus
the sense of community, conversation, and respect for our respec-
tive cultures; the imposition of consumerism by imitation of foreign
styles of life, versus the affirmation of our own Caribbean values.

Davis thinks that many of the Caribbean cultural values have
been preserved in the church because they have found in the
church a sense of acceptance, of reinterpretation of traditional values in the light of modernization, of respect and response. In many
of the territories, the churches have stood on the side of the less
privileged people, and very often some church leaders have been
criticized or harassed by governments because of their prophetic
stance in favor of the people. Davis makes the striking remark that
while in most of the West culture is the carrier of religion, in the
Caribbean, religions are the carrier of culture.

A theological understanding of our history of struggles for full
emancipation shows that our struggles are part of God's work of liberation within history. God is always the one who sets the captives
free. We can dare to hope that in spite of the political frustrations, external debt, structural adjustment, etc., God empowers us
to struggle as part of the people to bring for all the time of the Ju-
bilee (Luke 4:18–19), to make a reality this "Manifesto of Nazareth"
and Mary's "Magnificat" (Luke 1:46–55).

Caribbean Ecumenism

As the Caribbean islands started to become independent, from Haiti
in 1804 to St. Kitts-Nevis in 1983, efforts began to create structures
of cooperation and eventually of union, starting, of course, with the
British West Indies. Likewise, as the local churches became auton-
omous, some patriarchs of Caribbean ecumenism had the vision of
creating structures of collaboration and spiritual emulation.

In 1957, the then International Missionary Council, which was
instrumental in the creation of many regional councils of churches,
convened in Puerto Rico a Caribbean consultation, which was the
first meeting of its kind. Out of it developed the Caribbean Committee on Joint Christian Action (CCJCA), which guided projects for

the study of the Caribbean family and non-Christian religions and set up programs of communications training, youth development, and socioeconomic development. The latter was called Christian Action for Development in the Eastern Caribbean (CADEC) and was the impulse to found the United Theological College of the West Indies in Jamaica. Other ecumenical programs followed, and the need for a wider ecumenical body was felt. In 1970, a steering committee met in Jamaica to study the possibility of establishing a Caribbean conference of churches. CADEC was an earlier idea of the CCLA (Committee on Cooperation for Latin America, now Committee on the Caribbean and Latin America) as it searched for a more efficient way of helping in the region, more integrative and with fewer duplications.

In 1971 in Chaguaramas, Trinidad, CADEC organized the Caribbean Consultation for Development, an important milestone in the development of ecumenism in the region. Development was accepted by the churches as an integral part of the church's mission. One of the resolutions was to found a council of churches. Another important decision of the Chaguaramas consultation (which shows the political importance of the Caribbean Conference of Churches and the political involvement of the churches) was to recommend that the churches ask their governments to establish full diplomatic relations with Cuba. Barbados, Guyana, Trinidad and Tobago, and Jamaica were the first to establish relations in the whole continent, apart from Canada and Mexico, contributing in that way to create the necessary climate of respect for the self-determination of the peoples.

Two years later, on November 13, 1973, the Caribbean Conference of Churches was established in Kingston, with eighteen founding members, among them the Antilles Episcopal Conference of the Roman Catholic Church. At present there are thirty-four member churches, representing thirty-three Caribbean countries, practically all the region, and the different language areas. The Rev. Roy G. Neehall, a Presbyterian minister from Trinidad and Tobago, was elected as first general secretary. The second general secretary, Rev. Allan Kirton, a Methodist minister from Trinidad, served from 1983 to 1992. Elected in 1992 was the third general secretary, Edward Robert St. John Cumberbatch, a Methodist layperson from Barbados.

The preamble to the constitution of the CCC reads,

We as Christian people of the Caribbean, separated from each other by barriers of history, language, culture, class and distance, desire, because of our common calling in Christ, to join together in a regional fellowship of churches for inspiration, consultation and cooperative action. We are deeply concerned to promote the human liberation of our people, and are committed to the achievement of social justice and the dignity of man in our society. We desire to build up together our life in Christ and to share our experience for the mutual strengthening of the Kingdom of God in the World.

The Caribbean Conference of Churches has held five general assemblies. The theme of the inaugural one was "The Right Hand of God," using the hymn with the same title, which has become throughout the years the very symbol of the CCC. It was held in Jamaica in November 1973. In its message to the churches of the regions, the assembly delegates said: "As Dr. Philip Potter reminded us, how powerfully the message of our theme, 'The Right Hand of God,' has been fulfilled in our Caribbean history. As our survival out of the wretched past had been made possible, so our future with all its hopes and promises will be made certain." They ended with these words: "We, as Caribbean people and as Christian communities, must seek ways whereby we may ensure a more just use of power in the area that will lead towards the full human development of all persons and communities... so that we can attest to the power of the Right Hand of God as we attempt to fulfill our common commitment and live out our witness to our Lord Jesus Christ." The message was signed by the presidents: the Roman Catholic Archbishop S. E. Carter of Jamaica, Mrs. Dorinda Sampath, a Presbyterian layperson from Trinidad, and the Rev. Claude L. Cadogan, a Methodist pastor from Jamaica.

The second general assembly was held in Georgetown, Guyana, in November 1977, under the theme, "Workers Together with Christ." The three main subthemes focused on working together with Christ for human rights, for full human development, and for Caribbean unity. The elected praesidium for that year was the Roman Catholic archbishop of Trinidad, the Most Rev. Anthony Pantin; the Rt. Rev. Neville de Souza, Anglican bishop of Jamaica, and Mrs. Sampath again.

The third general assembly was held in Willemstad, Curaçao,

in November 1981, under the theme "Thine Is the Kingdom, the Power and the Glory." Francisco Reus Froylán, Episcopal bishop of Puerto Rico, wrote in the preparatory study booklet,

> Christ is the power of the powerless. When the church acts prophetically, renouncing privileges and comforts within the oppressive system, denouncing instances of injustice and exploitation, only then can we announce the coming of the new community of equity, radical sharing and mutual esteem; then the powerless begin to hope, to organize, to struggle.

The final message to member churches stated:

> But in God's plan for the establishment of his Kingdom, he has called Christians to partake in his power and to be his human agents in preparing for the gift of his Kingdom. . . . Ecumenical action on behalf of the Kingdom of God, utilizing God's power which comes from the Holy Spirit, can no longer be seen as an option for our churches. At this Assembly, member churches committed themselves to regional collaboration and to joint actions along the lines upon which we agree. But of greater urgency is ecumenical action in the national level within Christian Councils, where action to promote truth, goodness, justice, love and peace can be most concrete.

The presidents elected were Mrs. Joan Jones, an Anglican layperson from Trinidad, Mr. Paul Doth, a Moravian layperson from Suriname, and the Most Rev. Kelvin Felix, Roman Catholic archbishop of St. Lucia.

The fourth general assembly met in Barbados in September 1986, under the theme, "Jesus Christ: Justice, Hope, Peace." The elected presidents were the Rev. Richmond Nelson (Disciples of Christ, Jamaica); the Rt. Rev. Drexel Gomez, the Anglican bishop of Barbados, and Mrs. Myrtha Leetz-Cyntje, a Roman Catholic layperson from Curaçao.

The message to the churches this time stated:

> There is abundant evidence that there are many forms of injustice in the Caribbean, both in the interpersonal dimensions and as a structural reality. In a region in which so many people live without hope in situations of poverty, hunger, malnutrition and other distortions of our common life, the churches in the

Caribbean need to be concerned not merely in an intellectual way. We need to be prophetic in identifying the root causes of these things and to work conscientiously towards removing them. . . .

Many of our member churches in the Caribbean have had a great and noble tradition of social and political involvement. Some churches played their part in the slave emancipation one hundred and fifty years ago at a time when such a position was not a popular one. In spite of the fact that many people within the churches themselves wished for the *status quo* to remain, as did the constituted authorities, many churchmen were willing to take the unpopular stand for human libera-tion as an imperative of the Gospel. Today, we affirm that they were right. Reflecting on that period of our history in the Car-ibbean, the member churches of the Caribbean Conference of Churches need to note two things.

Firstly, human beings are in bondage in the Caribbean when unjust structures exist and when they have to live under the threat of militarization and nuclearization of the Caribbean. The imperative of the Gospel is that we must speak clearly as churches against this kind of bondage. Secondly, we need to remind ourselves that in the pre-emancipation period, as subse-quently, many churches in the Caribbean often were less than true to the Gospel because they abdicated their prophetic role in the face of many injustices, many situations which dimmed human hope, and much that did not make for peace.

The fifth general assembly was held in August 1991 in Port-of-Spain, Trinidad and Tobago, under the theme "Participants in God's World: Preserve–Renew–Recreate." The presidents elected were the Rev. Dr. Kingsley Lewis, a Moravian pastor from Antigua, Mrs. Leetz-Cyntje, and the Rev. Bruce Swapp, a Methodist pastor from Jamaica. In the message to the churches, the assembly said:

You have in the past been urged to involve yourselves in com-munity efforts and in nation-building, to raise your voices boldly against all forms of discrimination and corruption in public life and to exercise your franchise to the limit. All of this we wish to repeat and to endorse. Confronted as we are by new forms of delinquency as well in adults as in youth, the es-calation of the divorce rate, the glamorization of the worst and coarsest features of social life in the media, the rise of prostitution and venereal diseases, the widespread epidemic of HIV infection and of substance abuse, and the growing disenchantment with the political process as the avenue for meaningful change, we call upon you to do more for Christ than go to church. Be the salt of the earth! Be the light of the world! This is what we are expected to be!...

We appeal to you to be more alert to wanton destruction, pollution, litter, unsanitary conditions and the disposal of toxic wastes. We urge you both to stretch your hands and raise your voices for the healing of the land and the health of the people. Be a part of every good cause which is dedicated to peace and justice, community-building and the awakening of political consciousness. Do not be afraid! Encourage your pastors also to speak loudly and to act boldly when the safety of the people, the welfare of the community or the integrity of the nation is imperiled. Act in concert if you can, act alone if you must, but act! The time has come for the church to make the difference between what is and what ought to be!

Another important element in the ecumenical development of the region is the creation of National Christian Councils, many of them the result of visits of John R. Mott, a Methodist layperson from the United States and one of the great patriarchs of ecumenism. The Jamaica Council of Churches was established in 1941, as was the Cuban Council of Churches (now the Cuban Ecumenical Council).

The Mandate of the Caribbean Conference of Churches

The Mandate of the CCC, which was approved in August 1985, summarized the objectives of the institution in the following terms: "Ecumenism and social change in obedience to Jesus Christ and in solidarity with the poor." This is also the best summary of "Caribbean Emancipation Theology."

1. "Ecumenism," this great dimension of contemporary Christianity, is seen in the region to include "Caribbean integration." We can affirm that all the first patriarchs of the independence of different territories shared a vision of a final integration of the whole region that goes beyond our insularity and fragmentation. This, therefore, affirms our cultural identity against the foreign cultural

penetration of the powerful media; it affirms our history of struggles, frustrations, and achievements in human rights and the quality of life. Not much progress has been accomplished in the actual union of churches of different traditions, but more important than that we feel is that in the Caribbean at the grassroots, Catholic and Protestant people can work together to face the great political and social challenges of the present day (John 17, Gal. 3:28).

2. "Social change" is defined in one of the CCC documents presented to the fourth assembly: "The call to social change is a call to the churches – the Christian community – for engagement in a ministry of challenge to, and transformation of, the religious, moral, cultural, social, economic, and political structures and root causes which prevent the people of the region from making their fullest contribution to the development process." This concept of "social change," which is very dynamic, defines what we understand by the much-used word "development." In this same document, we read: "Development is understood as a process of liberation in which the poor themselves become active agents once they are aware that they possess the power to transform those structures and those aspects of reality which inhibit them." And we call "conscientization" – borrowing the term from our Latin American brothers and sisters and particularly from Paulo Freire's "liberation pedagogy" – our educational process by which we guide them to understand their situation and to empower them to change it. That was the origin of the first English Caribbean Christian education curriculum, "Christian Living Series," and more adequately so in the second curriculum, "Fashion Me a People" (Matt. 5:13–14), so ably directed by Dr. Joyce Bailey, a Methodist educator from Jamaica who is a professor at the United Theological College, University of the West Indies, in Jamaica.

3. "Solidarity with the poor": The nice word "solidarity" came to us from politics, but the same concept is straightforward in the Bible. It is the word *koinonia* – communion. An excellent Spanish version of the Bible translates the phrase in the "apostolic benediction" as "the solidarity of the Holy Spirit." From the documents of CELAM (the Latin American Roman Catholic Bishops Conference) the Vatican and other church leaders have taken the phrase "option for the poor," which means that God has made a covenant with the poor, assigning them a very special role in the history of liberation. If we have poor, it is because of wrong politics and wrong economics, which create the class distinctions that keep making the rich

richer and the poor poorer. The same document states: "The call to a ministry in solidarity with the poor reminds the Christian community that the biblical message and the ongoing historical role of the church calls for a constant identification with those persons in our societies who are most inhibited in their struggle for justice and in their striving to live a life of peace" (Luke 6:20; James 2:5-6).

4. In "obedience to Jesus Christ": "Obedience" is a difficult concept in the Caribbean. It makes us recall slavery; so often the slaves bowed down to the master, saying, "Yes, backra massa!" (yes, white master). Obedience to Jesus is based on the obedience of Jesus himself (Phil. 2:6-11), the obedience of him who surrendered his life for others in service and sacrifice. So in the same way, our obedience is obedience within the grace, in a relation of love and not of imposition, obedience in the sense of discipleship (Mark 8:34-35). We follow Jesus, "going to him outside the camp,... seeking the New Jerusalem," the new "polis" for the Caribbean (Heb. 13:12-14). The CCC Fourth Assembly document on social change ends thus: "This commitment and action arise from and are squarely based upon our call to *faithful engagement with Jesus Christ* in obedience to his demands and His leadership, especially in respect of his own uncompromising bias towards the poor."

Perspectives into the Future

- The CCC has to be more self-supported. The churches have to see the CCC more as their own enterprise. More churches have to enrich the fellowship within the CCC, particularly the Charismatic and Pentecostal communities, which have grown in the region so tremendously.

- More efforts should be pursued to engage churches of different traditions in dialogue toward possible organic union and widespread discussion on "faith and order" issues. We have to share with other regions the almost unique experience of Roman Catholic active participation.

- The Christian churches have to study the phenomenon of popular religiosity, neo-African cults such as the "Ras Tafari," the "spiritual Baptists" in Trinidad and Barbados, "Winti" in Suriname, etc. The large Hindu and Islamic communities call for a better climate of understanding and collaboration in the region as well.

- The growing network of regional NGOs presents us with an alternative to the failures of governments in the region more and more affected because of the structural adjustments that limit their resources for social programs for the benefit of the poor and disenfranchised.

- In the socio-political field, our peoples will be facing great challenges that will demand more concerted actions from the governments, NGOs, and churches. Two main factors are affecting the quality of life of the Caribbean peoples: the external debt, which takes a lot of resources that could have been used to benefit the people to service the debt, and the structural adjustments proposed by the World Bank and the International Monetary Fund with the same injuries to the people.

13

Mission Impossible?

by Dale A. Bisnauth

Aided and abetted by the Christian capacity for hope, it struck me that a North-South cooperative venture in mission holds out exciting possibilities.

A joint approach to mission will demand of all of us – Christians of North America as well as Christians of the Caribbean – a capacity to transcend our parochialism and to think in global terms. This is vastly easier said than done, given our histories, traditions, and other factors that have shaped our attitudes.

Ask yourselves: How can churches of the North which are institutions within politically powerful countries, with a tradition for "giving" and "sending" as far as mission is concerned, work in tandem with churches of the Caribbean that are institutions within politically and economically fragile countries, with a tradition for "receiving"? How can they work in a way that will do justice to the integrity of all the churches concerned and, what is more, promote the mission of the church?

Permit me to personalize some of the issues involved in the rather large question. Not so long ago, I was privileged to go on a speaking tour across Canada organized by the Ecumenical Forum. Invariably – I mean *invariably* – when I was finished giving my spiel on the church in the Caribbean, the first question I was asked was "What can we do to help you people?" or words to that effect. I have no doubt that folks were genuinely interested in us Caribbean peoples and that the question was provoked by a genuine desire to be helpful to us in our work.

But after the sixth such query, I lost my temper (which, I admit I should not have done) and the questions just rushed out: "Why is it that you always feel that you can *do* something for us? Why can't you just be there for us?" Why do you want to make us the object of your charity, and use our plight to score brownie points for yourselves? We don't want your charity; we simply want justice. Are you really prepared to help us get that?"

The silence that followed my outburst was thunderous. Finally, an older woman asked: "Why have you come to talk to us? We thought it was to solicit our help. And you did sound as if you are doing just that." I was under the impression that I was just sharing stories, impressions, and concerns of the church in the Caribbean. But looking back now, I am certain that I emphasized the concern more than anything else and must have sounded as if I were soliciting financial and other assistance for overseas missionary projects.

Here is another vignette, which may indicate what a tradition for receiving has done to our thinking.

Several years ago, I represented the Caribbean Conference of Churches at a Partners-in-Mission Conference hosted by the Anglican Province of the West Indies. Episcopalian and Anglican bishops (and their advisors) from Canada, Britain, and the United States were in attendance. Not even this hypercritical nonconformist was prepared for what happened. This Partners-in-Mission event was nothing more than Caribbean ecclesiastics presenting for discussion and acceptance "shopping lists" of needs ranging from stationery and typewriter ribbons to funding for a theological college!

One would have thought that the "Partners-in-Mission" would have sought to identify issues of major concern like the Haitian refugee problem, free and fair elections in Guyana, human rights violations in Suriname, the effects of tourism on Antigua, the external debt burden facing the Caribbean, the problem of the escalating abuse of narcotic substances in North America and the Caribbean, emigration/immigration and its implications for mission, and so on. And then go on to make concrete decisions as to what joint missional projects/programs could be launched to bring the Christian gospel to bear on these human conditions of personal and institutional sin.

But the conference discussed shopping lists! One did not know whether to laugh or to cry! A significant thing was that the overseas partners seemed impatient over the "shopping-list" approach to joint mission. But nobody said so. They were probably very conscious of the fact that mission and missionaries of the past had been accused by Caribbean church leaders of being paternalistic, patronizing, and arrogant. It seemed as if they did not want to be similarly accused. That in itself is part of the problem.

Overseas missionaries in the past were quite clear as to their goals; and, by and large, they achieved those goals. Judged by modern standards, their assumptions might not have been always right, their methods might not have been always correct. But they got the job done. Today, the fear that the church may be wrong in its missional assumptions and methods cripples it into near inactivity. Instead of forgiving the past, learning from its mistakes, and getting on with the responsibility of being the church in these times, the church allows the guilt over yesteryear to get it bogged down unnecessarily.

We in the Caribbean cannot forget the *encomienda* system by which the indigenous Indians were decimated; we cannot forget the attitude of the established church towards slavery and emancipation; we cannot forget the missionary thrusts into these parts that were the religio-cultural reflex of Manifest Destiny and the "White Man's Burden," and so on. Perhaps we should not forget these things. But the memory of them should not make us bitter or cynical; and it should not make us suspicious of North Americans who are Christians like ourselves.

Why should we believe that contemporary North Americans share the assumptions of their forebears in the faith? Why should we believe that they are American and Canadian "imperialists" first and Christians only by accident? Do we not believe that the Christian faith has the power to enable us all to rise above the politics that would polarize us into First World–Third World, superpower-oppressed relationships?

Meanwhile, I would suggest that the churches in North America should treat us as if we have come of age, as people whose prejudices should not be pampered, and as people who can rise above the temptation to be so politically identified with the past that they cannot be open to new possibilities in relationships with North American church-folk.

We would hope that you are theologically mature enough not to so identify with your country that you cannot distinguish between your loyalty to Jesus Christ and your allegiance to your politics. Theological maturity will enable you to appreciate that, more often than not, Caribbean peoples are peeved at your governmental policies in this region and not against North Americans as such. It will enable us to appreciate that Christians in North America do not necessarily share the stance of their governments in relation to the Caribbean or elsewhere.

But that maturity does not come by happenstance or by good will. We have to work at it and work at it ecumenically. By "ecumenically" here I do not only mean across denominational lines; I mean geographical lines as well. If our partnership in mission is to be real, we had better begin to reflect on missiology together even prior to our planning together for mission to North America and to the Caribbean and possibly Latin America. If we reflect together, Caribbean persons may well surprise themselves when they come to appreciate how much they have to contribute in insights, information, and theology. We may be lacking in financial resources, but that does not mean that we have nothing to contribute in a process of dialogue and sharing.

Actually, any project or program in which North American and Caribbean church persons will be involved will not constitute a first. We have had such sharing in the past. We can benefit from the experiences we have had together and, hopefully, avoid some of the mistakes that were made in the past.

The United Theological College of the West Indies came about some twenty-odd years ago as the result of close cooperation between North American churches (Canada and the United States) and Caribbean churches. The value of this ecumenical training institution to the Caribbean church cannot be overemphasized. To be sure, at first the only things "Caribbean" about UTCWI were the fact that it was located in Jamaica, a Caribbean island, the fact that the students were from the region, and the fact that in its physical layout the campus resembled a slave plantation! The courses taught and the lecturers were, in the main, from outside the region. Wardens ensured that whatever denominational emphases were modified during class hours were restored come Monday morning at confessional classes. Another cause for complaint has been the fact that around 60 percent of the persons trained for ministries in the Caribbean at UTCWI have migrated to Canada and the United States. Maybe this provides us with an indication as to the relevance of the UTCWI training for the Caribbean!

Then, the Caribbean Conference of Churches came about as the result of further cooperation between North American churches and their Caribbean counterparts. Even before the CCC was formally constituted, North American churches strongly supported ecumenical undertakings and programs out of which the CCC grew. One such program was the Caribbean Committee on Joint Christian Action (CCJCA), which published the first indigenously produced Christian education curriculum for the region. Another program was known as Christian Action for Development in the Eastern Caribbean (CADEC). In fact, the decision to initiate CADEC was taken by the Committee on Middle America and the Caribbean of the Latin American Department of Church World Service (now Church World Service and Witness), part of the National Council of Churches of Christ in the United States of America.

The emphasis on "development" as the new name for "mission," which informs much of the work of the CCC, reflects the thinking of Church World Service. Theologically, that thinking has helped the main-line or ecumenically oriented churches of the region to break out of the pietism that informed much of their life and practice.

Today, churches of Canada and the United States provide funding for the CCC's work. The United Church of Canada is most exemplary in that it does not designate its funds. That is, it does not say what program its funds are to be used for. Churches of the United States provide support through the CWSW, although some also provide additional support directly. I must confess a personal preference for support through the ecumenical agency. Maybe that is because of my preference for ecumenism and my impatience over denominationalism, which, in my estimation, is too divisive of small Caribbean states and too much of a reminder that it is part of our colonial legacy.

One of the most exciting models of North-South cooperation in mission to emerge in recent times has been the São Paulo Process. I had the privilege of participating in the São Paulo event in May 1986. The process involves Latin American, North American, and Caribbean persons in joint reflection on hemispheric political, social, and economic issues from a theological perspective, in planning and budgeting, in project/program implementation, and in evaluation. Missional programs take place as much in North America as in Latin America and the Caribbean.

The São Paulo Process has demonstrated that mission that is ecumenical across denominational and geographical boundaries, that involves a sharing of resources in terms of persons, expertise, in-sights, and money, that perceives of mission as moving as much from the South to the North as the other way round, that seeks to bring the gospel of the Rule of God to address issues such as injus-tice against women and children, refugees, indigenous peoples, and so on, is possible. But it demands will, commitment, generosity of spirit, and, above all, love for Jesus Christ and God's Rule.